STEAMING INTO BEDFORDSHIRE

Before the diesel era. Standard Class 4 4-6-0 No. 75040 coasts into the south end of Luton Midland Road station with a local train to Bedford on Tuesday 8 April 1959.
(*S. Summerson*)

Front endpaper (left)
Two ancient locomotives undergo repairs in Wellingborough's roundhouse on Saturday 3 July 1937. Ex-Midland Railway 2-4-0 No. 20266 (1881) has had its leading driving wheels removed for attention, and 1798 class 0-6-0 No. 3566 (1897) has similarly lost its centre driving wheels. (*H. C. Casserley*)

Front endpaper (right)
Bletchley's 4F 0-6-0 No. 44447 draws in to Fenny Stratford platform running light engine and brake from the Bedford direction on Saturday 11 January 1958. (*H. C. Casserley*)

Title page
Streamlined A4 Pacifc No. 60003 "Andrew K. McKosh" speeds through Sandy station with the 09.40 King's Cross to Newcastle-upon-Tyne express on Bank Holiday Monday 7 August 1961. (*Michael Mensing*)

Rear endpaper (left)
The rarely photographed Newport Pagnell station was host to ex-LNWR 0-6-2T No. 58887 with the push-pull train from Wolverton on Thursday 16 October 1952. (*A. J. Pike*)

Rear endpaper (right)
A 4-2-2 'Spinner' and a 4-4-0 double-head a passenger train northwards away from Bedford and pass under the station signal gantry in Midland Railway days. (*Bill Davies collection*)

Class 5 4-6-0 No. 44873 of Bescot shed rests momentarily at the north end of Bletchley station with a down local train on Saturday 10 October, 1959.   (*H. C. Casserley*)

STEAMING
INTO BEDFORDSHIRE

by
DAVID EATWELL

W. D. WHARTON
Wellingborough

First published in 2001 by
W. D. Wharton
37 Sheep Street
Wellingborough
Northamptonshire NN8 1BX

Text copyright © David Eatwell 2001

David Eatwell asserts his moral right
to be identified as the author of this work

ISBN 1-899597-15-8

Dedicated to the memory of
F. G. (Fred) Cockman

Designed and typeset by John Hardaker, Wollaston, Northamptonshire
Printed and bound in Great Britain by
Butler & Tanner Ltd
Frome, Somerset

CONTENTS

Belpaire-boilered Prince of Wales class 4-6-0 No. 25827 rests in Bletchley shed on Saturday 21 May 1938.   (*Les Hanson*)

RAILWAY LINES
IN AND AROUND BEDFORDSHIRE

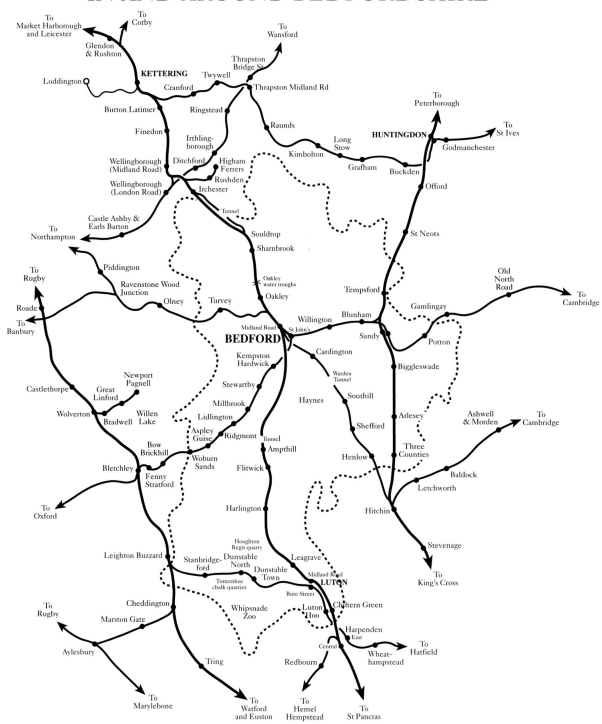

FOREWORD

by F. G. Cockman

This is the second of David Eatwell's excellent books on railways in the Bedfordshire area. They are an invaluable pictorial record of the great days of steam which came to an end in 1968.

My own interest in railways could be said to have begun in 1906 when my father, himself a railway enthusiast, used to take me in the train to Stratford station. Here, on Platform 7, one could see not only express engines returning to depot but also locomotives in their workshop grey livery, newly erected and awaiting their first trial run. Thus, at the early age of 4, I could appreciate the handsome lines of the Claud Hamilton 4-4-0s in their shining Prussian blue.

Two other interesting types were rebuilds of James Holden's famous T19 2-4-0s. One retained its wheel arrangement but carried a large Belpaire boiler resulting in a rather ungainly appearance. They were called 'Humpty Dumpties'. The other rebuild was a 4-4-0 resembling a Claud Hamilton but having a single side window cab. Many of these engines ran for some time in their workshop livery and were referred to as 'Dolly Grays'. Holden's freight engines were also of attractive appearance, notably his G58 0-6-0s (LNER J17).

In 1921 I made my first acquaintance with the Midland Railway which has been my favourite ever since. I travelled daily from Leytonstone to King's Cross (widened lines) and thus became familiar with the work of the Kirtley and the Johnson 0-4-4Ts. The Kirtleys were, in my opinion, the stronger of the two and a Johnson example was preserved for many years. Unfortunately it was cut up during the Stanier regime.

My railway experience was enlarged in 1933 when I moved to Potters Bar. For the next five years I was able to see the best products of Doncaster in action, such as the Gresley A3s and A4s. The latter, of course, hauled the famous 'Silver Jubilee' express which was extremely popular with the travelling public. In 1934 the P2 2-8-2 class appeared. This had been designed for the Aberdeen service and the engines were 'run in' on stopping trains between King's Cross and Hitchin. These trains were a bonus for suburban passengers.

In 1938 I moved to Bedford and thus renewed my acquaintance with the Midland, now part of the London Midland & Scottish Railway. At that time the fastest trains were worked by the Jubilees with secondary duties in the hands of the Compounds, the Class 2 4-4-0s and an occasional 'Belpaire'. Goods trains, or freight as they are now called, were entrusted to the Class 3 or 4 0-6-0s according to weight restrictions. Perhaps the best sight of all was a Beyer-Garratt at the head of 80 wagons of coal on the long climb from Bedford to milepost 34.

The war years soon followed and here tribute must be paid to the thousands of enginemen who had to cope with worn out locomotives, poor quality fuel, constant blackouts and air-raid damage. It can truly be said that on the home front the railways won the war.

For the railway enthusiast the years immediately following 1948 were full of interest. Between the years 1951 and 1954 British Railways through the Railway Executive produced 12 new designs. Of these the Class 5 4-6-0 stayed only a short time, but the Class 4 4-6-0 (75000) and 2-6-4T (80000) stayed for several years. Bedford loco men also took their turn with the Class 9 2-10-0 which had displaced the Beyer-Garratts from the coal trains.

Admiration of the steam engine leads inevitably to a wish to travel on the footplate and I was fortunate in knowing Cyril Palmer, Motive Power Superintendent at King's Cross, who was very generous with passes. I thus gained an intimate knowledge of the working of the Gresley A3 and the Peppercorn A1 Pacifics. For their part, the London Midland Region had a sense of humour, and one footplate pass arrived with the instruction, "Present yourself at Bletchley Loco at 3 a.m. to travel on the 4 a.m. to Banbury." On this journey I was able to admire the way in which the driver shunted wagons at Buckingham yard in pitch darkness with perfect accuracy. The engine was a Class 4 4-6-0.

I much appreciate having been asked to write this foreword. Although steam has been absent from the national network for over 30 years, the interest in steam engines is as strong as ever and I am sure that this second book of David Eatwell's will be as successful as the first.

F. G. Cockman

INTRODUCTION

In my book *Railway Nostalgia Around Bedfordshire* I made a conscious effort to cover as much as possible of the Bedfordshire steam scene and to make the captions as informative as space permitted. Each railway line was dealt with (more or less geographically) and from the book's 40,000-plus words a fairly extensive history of the lines and their locomotives emerged.

To a degree it continues here, but this book is more a collection of some of the best photographs taken within the county (and just beyond) by some of the best railway photographers ever to have wielded their cameras in the area … plus a few by the author! Also included are some historical scenes, some more examples of pleasure railways and another look at industrial railways.

Overall, *Steaming Into Bedfordshire* includes a comprehensive selection of photographs featuring all major (and most minor) railways in the Bedfordshire region. Most of the photographs have not been published before, and the few which have are included because of their great interest and quality.

Indeed, all the photographs have had to be strong in these attributes to qualify for inclusion, both in this and my previous book. Historical significance and high quality in all stages of production have been the goals. It is hoped the reader will feel that these objectives have been achieved again.

David Eatwell
Bedford

ACKNOWLEDGEMENTS

Although my name appears on the front cover, this is by no means a one man effort, and I must give credit here to the experts, photographers and other helpers, many of whom I am fortunate to be able to call friends, who have so willingly given their time and expertise to ensure not only that I kept to the straight and narrow, but also that I did not put my foot in it if it could at all be helped.

Obviously, only a few of the photographs are my own, so it would have been impossible to compile this later album without being able to tap into the work of many great names from the past whose photographic collections have been so lovingly cared for over the years. Individual photographers (where known) are credited at the end of each caption, but many are deceased, and it is the present custodians of this invaluable material who deserve special praise.

I do not wish to single out anyone for particular thanks because in their own way everyone with whom I have made contact during the last few months has made an indispensable contribution, so I hope the gentlemen whose names follow will accept these general thanks from me because, as I'm sure they realise, without them, the book could not possibly have been completed: Malcolm Burgoyne, Fred Cockman, Bryan Cross, Bill Davies, Chris Foren, Maurice Jeyes, Graham Leach, Steve Lacey, Dave Longman, Ray Schofield, Colin Stacey, Stephen Summerson and Robin Waywell. Also, to my great good fortune, I have gleaned a considerable amount of information through regular attendance at meetings (both locally and nationally) held by the Locomotive Club of Great Britain (LCGB).

Prominent amongst the many sources of reference I have used were: a selection of Ian Allan's *ABCs* and *Locoshed Books*, *Bedford*

ASLEF 80 Years by Bill Davies, *British Rail-Gradient Profiles* published by Ian Allan, *British Railways Sectional Maps (1947)* published by Ian Allan, *Gresley Pacifics* by R. M. Tufnell, *The Hatfield, Luton and Dunstable Railway* by Sue and Geoff Woodward, *An Illustrated History of LNWR Engines* by Edward (Ted) Talbot, *The Midland Railway, A Chronology* by John Gough, *Nameplates of the Big Four* by Frank Burridge, *Oxford to Cambridge Railway* by Bill Simpson, *Royal Scot* by C. J. Freezer, *Stanier Locomotives* by Brian Haresnape and *Steam Locomotives of British Railways* by H. C. Casserley.

As before, I drew inspiration from the railway books of Richard Coleman and Joe Rajczonek, also published by Robert Wharton of Wellingborough, and to him and editor John Hardaker I offer my thanks for allowing me the (almost!) free hand to prepare a book to my own personal taste. A favourite expression of Robert's is, 'The author always knows best – except when the publisher knows better!', and I consider myself lucky indeed that he so rarely felt it necessary even to suggest that he just might know better!

And finally, despite protestations to the contrary in the acknowledgements to *Railway Nostalgia Around Bedfordshire*, I have to admit (secretly, quite proudly) that I did eventually allow myself to be initiated into the mysteries of modern technology and that the manuscript of *Steaming Into Bedfordshire* was prepared on my (fairly) up-to-date computer instead of my steam-age typewriter, but not without a considerable struggle. With the book finished at last, perhaps I shall now be able to find the time to discover how to operate a PC properly!

David Eatwell

THE MIDLAND MAIN LINE
Wellingborough to Harpenden

In common with much of the network, railway infrastructure in the Wellingborough area has now been almost totally erased, but in steam days this was a major centre with large shed and extensive sidings – and a magnificent station, the north end of which is shown here. The sweeping curve and some of the buildings have survived, along with the ornate canopy over (some of) the down fast platform, but there is a 'new' foot-bridge, the style of which hardly blends in, and only one slow line remains with little else to remind us what an important railway town Wellingborough was. Completing the picture above is a view of a rare visitor to this part of the world in the shape of the named Class 5 4-6-0 No. 45156 "Ayrshire Yeomanry", at this time resident at Newton Heath shed, Manchester, and destined to be one of the last steam locomotives in service on British Railways. The train is in the down sidings and the date is Friday 31 May 1957.

(Ken Fairey)

The Midland Railway was well known for its double-heading policy, and it was therefore no surprise that this should continue into LMS days on ex-Midland territory. Even into nationalised British Railways the practice was perpetuated, and in the latter days of steam one of the most frequently seen combinations was a 2P 4-4-0 piloting a Jubilee 4-6-0. Here, just such a pair is caught passing Morris Motors Works, south of Wellingborough station, with an express for St Pancras on Tuesday 2 June 1959. The locomotives are No. 40632 of Nottingham shed and No. 45649 "Hawkins" of Derby.

(Ken Fairey)

The site of Irchester Junction was 1½ miles south of Wellingborough Station which itself is 65 miles north of St Pancras and has the 65-mile post actually at the station. The box controlled the connection to the Higham Ferrers branch which went off to the east (a line which finally closed at the end of 1969). Passing southwards at the head of one of the lengthy coal trains from Toton to Brent on Saturday 13 November 1965 is 8F 2-8-0 No. 48119, a member of one of the last steam classes to survive on British railways. They were Stanier's first major goods engines for the LMS and were a class whose numbers eventually filled the series between 48000 and 48775. So highly thought of were these 2-8-0s that during World War II examples were also built by the LNER, the GWR and the Southern Railway in their own workshops, as well as by private builders. 8Fs worked abroad too, notably in Egypt and Turkey, and were still in use in the 1990s in the latter country where they were nicknamed 'Churchills'.

(Ken Fairey)

11

LEFT With steam to spare, Nottingham-based 4F No. 43888 takes it easy on the descent from Sharnbrook Tunnel and heads south with a train of loose-coupled 16-ton loaded coal wagons on the same date as the photograph below. Regarded by many (but not all!) railwaymen as fairly useless machines, these 0-6-0s were introduced on to the Midland Railway in 1911 by Sir Henry Fowler and must have found favour in some quarters because the design was perpetuated later by the LMS. When production finally ceased in 1940, the total reached the dizzy heights of 772 locomotives, and 4Fs held the British record at that time for the most locomotives in a single class. Not bad for a flawed design!

(*Michael Mensing*)

RIGHT From the time of their introduction in 1935, 8F class 2-8-0s were a common sight on the Midland Main Line, and of the 666 taken into BR capital stock more than 150 were still in service at the beginning of 1968. Consequently, various examples have been preserved, and some of them have since returned to main line metals to haul enthusiasts' specials in numerous parts of the country. The Midland Main Line was one route in England where they excelled with the haulage of long and heavy coal trains between Toton and Brent, and on Monday 18 September 1961 No. 48490 of Toton shed was heading for home with a train of spoil. The photograph shows the locomotive on the down slow line near Sharnbrook and is on the route which goes through the tunnel rather than the more steeply graded line over the summit. This has been singled now, and most trains go 'over the top', but it is not out of use entirely, although passenger trains tend to go through only in emergencies, most steam specials excepted. (*Michael Mensing*)

Souldrop signal box stood adjacent to the up fast line near the southern end of the line through Sharnbrook Tunnel which is 1 mile 90 yards long and which was built to ease the journey of the long and heavy goods and mineral trains that for so many years laboured along this route from the Midlands to London. Kentish Town's Jubilee class 6P5F 4-6-0 No. 45561 "Saskatchewan" is not about to pass through the tunnel on the trip depicted here, however, as it is seen (on Thursday 24 April 1960) about to sweep past the 1920-built box on the down fast line; a position it will have held all the way from St Pancras. The signalman is seen enjoying the passage of the express from the open window of his cabin and probably hoping that the draught created by the fast-moving train will not knock over his motor-cycle which the photographer noticed was parked by the side of the line, just out of the picture to the right. (*Ken Fairey*)

Sharnbrook Station was almost seven miles north of Bedford and was opened for the use of passengers in May 1857. After a life of a few days short of 103 years, this amenity was withdrawn in May 1960, and as both Oakley and Irchester stations had been closed previously, when Sharnbrook 'died' there was then no station open on the 15-mile stretch of line between Bedford and Wellingborough. Half-hearted talk of re-opening one or other of these stations (Oakley has been the prime target) as a parkway to ease Bedford's ever-increasing traffic problems has surfaced at regular intervals, but, as the remaining buildings there are in private and commercial use, it is probable that any new station would need to be at a new site, which has become something of a stumbling block to the scheme. On Saturday 16 August 1958, Sharnbrook still retained its stopping trains, and here amidst the gas lamps and the typically Midland angled fencing, Standard Class 4 4-6-0 No. 75064 of Nottingham shed pauses in the up fast platform with a stopping train for St Pancras. Less than two years later, trains ceased to serve Sharnbrook, and today's passengers sweeping past on the Midland Main Line can be forgiven for not realising that there was ever a station here.

(*S. Summerson*)

In a setting which has changed little after 40 years, these two Midland Main Line scenes show goods trains that are about to pass under Bromham Road bridge from the north on Monday 18 September 1961.

RIGHT Stanier 8F 2-8-0 No. 48356 of Kettering shed is in charge of one of the lengthy coal trains which ran from Toton to Brent and which were such a common sight at this time. It will shortly be passing through Bedford on the up fast avoiding line and therefore it will not be going through the platforms of Bedford Midland Road station.

(*Michael Mensing*)

LEFT Fowler 4F 0-6-0 No. 44020 of Wellingborough plods along at a far more sedate pace than its eight-coupled cousin (above) with the first three wagons of its train containing sleepers and the rest full of coal, perhaps for local coal merchants rather than going to London as the 8F is doing. This train *will* go through the station platforms and may very well be held there for some time to allow faster trains to pass, which was a fate frequently to befall the Brent-bound coal trains. Such activity was not popular with trainspotters on the up side of the lines in the station area as it blocked their view of trains speeding through on the 'main', and thus many a potential 'cop' was missed, to the obvious consternation of those concerned.

(*Michael Mensing*)

15

Ivatt 2-6-2T No. 41270 tops up from the water-column at the southern end of Bedford Midland Road station's No. 3 platform on Saturday 24 September 1955. In view of the fact that the locomotive is fitted for push-pull working, that there are only two coaches in the consist and that there is a single headcode lamp at the top of the smoke box, it is reasonable to assume that the train will shortly be moving into one of the bay platforms for a trip to Northampton. This extremely attractive and atmospheric station was swept away in a wave of destruction in 1978 to be replaced by the modernistic structure which today occupies a site some hundred yards to the north – but, then, that's progress! (*H. C. Casserley*)

Bedford shed was conveniently placed in the area between the River Great Ouse and the Midland Road station, although locomotives coming off trains in the station had to undertake a conflicting manoeuvre and cross the up and down main lines in order to retreat to the confines of the shed. Known to older enthusiasts as 15D but to younger ones as 14E, Bedford motive power depot is behind the photographer in this view of Standard Class 5 No. 73156 heading northwards with a fitted express goods train on Tuesday 23 May 1961. An overall view of the shed area in colour is shown on page 155. *(R. J. White)*

STEAMING INTO BEDFORDSHIRE

Ampthill Tunnel (and its immediate environs) was a joyous place to watch the trains in steam days. There were bridges overlooking the mouths of the two bores at both ends, and although it might involve a little walking at the southern end, it is still possible to peer through the overhead wires at the entrances (and exits) today as both bridges have survived through all the modernisation programmes that have been implemented since these photographs were taken. Those on this page were taken off the private bridge to the north and the photographs on the page opposite were taken off another (but much grander) private bridge to the south. The gradient favours down trains here so photographers preferred those on the up lines in the hope that they would provide better smoke effects, but it didn't always work out that way as is demonstrated by the different amounts of exhaust visible in these four photographs taken in the summer of 1960 (those on this page at lunchtime and on the page opposite in late afternoon).

ABOVE An unidentified Black Five 4-6-0 heads a semi-fast train northwards out of the tunnel.
(*David Eatwell*)

LEFT Nottingham-based Jubilee 4-6-0 No. 45650 "Blake" is on its way to St Pancras, demonstrating near-perfect combustion as it passes Millbrook up the 1 in 200 climb. Ironically, the locomotive working uphill shows little exhaust whilst the locomotive taking it easy down the grade shows a respectable stream of smoke. (*David Eatwell*)

RIGHT Another unidentified locomotive, this time a Jubilee class 4-6-0, is shortly to enter the tunnel with a fast train for the north, so it is nice to see something issuing from both the chimney and the safety-valve of the locomotive. At the back of the train, the bridge (now demolished) over the line which provided the only road access to Ampthill station is just about visible through the exhaust smoke.   (*David Eatwell*)

LEFT Jubilee class 4-6-0 No. 45575 "Madras" is in its usual immaculate condition as it powers a train for St Pancras out of the tunnel just as a pair of the newly-introduced Rolls Royce DMUs for Bedford pass on the down slow. The beautiful exhaust from "Madras" is no surprise as the train is pounding up the 1 in 200 incline.   (*David Eatwell*)

STEAMING INTO BEDFORDSHIRE

The photographs on the previous page were taken from the five-arch occupation bridge which spans the four tracks of the Midland Main Line between the southern portals of Ampthill Tunnel and the site of Ampthill station (see opposite), little sign of which now remains. The bridge still stands, however, and is shown in both these photographs of goods trains on the up slow line on Saturday 16 July 1955.

RIGHT Here, unrebuilt Crosti 9F 2-10-0 No. 92026 of Wellingborough shed is giving a good demonstration of one reason why these locomotives were so unpopular; the smoke from the side chimney used to blow down and obscure the view from the footplate.
(*T. E. Rounthwaite*)

LEFT Stanier 8F 2-8-0 No. 48191, also of Wellingborough, is making light work of its mixed goods train up the 1 in 200 gradient (which exists over much of the route between Bedford and Leagrave) as can be seen by the steam escaping from the safety valve. Both footplate crews will be mightily relieved to be out in the open again after being in the confined space of the smoke-filled tunnel with the resultant lack of fresh air, but that was an accepted way of life on the railway in steam days and something all footplate men had to learn to put up with.
(*T. E. Rounthwaite*)

When this photograph was taken in early 1959, Ampthill station had but a short time left to live and was already in a state of considerable disrepair as can be seen by the lack of canopy on the down fast platform into which the train is running. There had been a station here since the London Extension opened in 1868, but in railway terms 91 years is not a particularly long time for a station to last and Ampthillonians were naturally 'up in arms' when closure was announced. In this photograph, Black Five 4-6-0 No. 45221 of Bedford shed is trundling in with a stopping train from St Pancras, but it won't be doing that many more times because the threatened closure was to come the following May amid much wailing, gnashing of teeth, and a rendition of *Abide With Me* on the platform. All attempts to effect a re-opening failed, of course, and another piece of important railway history was lost forever. (*T. E. Rounthwaite*)

LEFT A common occurrence on the Midland Main Line. Although mainly out of sight in this photograph, the train will consist of the usual eight or nine coaches (platforms along the line could not accommodate any more). Passing near Steppingley (between Ampthill and Flitwick) it is heading towards St Pancras on a very windy day in the early 1950s. The Nottingham-shedded class 2P 4-4-0 No. 40454 is the pilot, and the Jubilee with the straight-sided tender (possibly No. 45612 "Jamaica") was one of only a handful to work along here in that condition at the time. Unfortunately the details were not recorded so we shall never know for sure just what it was. *(Peter Chapman)*

RIGHT Not such a common sight were two 8F 2-8-0s double-heading a train along the Midland Main Line and seen here overtaking a Compound 4-4-0 just south of Ampthill station, possibly on the same date in the early 1950s as the photograph (top) in view of the high wind blowing here too. The 8Fs will probably be taking empty coal-wagons back to Toton from Brent, and since a single 8F was quite capable of coping with as many empties as could fit into a block section, the reason for the double heading here is most likely to save one of the locomotives occupying a path on its own. Even with four tracks, the Midland Main Line had very little spare capacity so such a move would be encouraged by the controllers. The Compound 4-4-0 on the passenger train looks as if it is just coasting in for a stop in the station, so the photographer must indeed have counted his blessings when such a photo-opportunity presented itself. Some people have all the luck, don't they? *(Peter Chapman)*

Harlington goods yard in LMS days; Wednesday 7 June 1939. Most stations along the Midland Main Line had their own goods yards almost from their inception, and overall dealt with a vast amount of local traffic. Virtually none of these yards still exists, but their sites may usually be located by present-day car parks, a sad reflection on the times. The locomotive doing a bit of shunting here is No. 3967 and is one of the 192 original Midland 4F class of 0-6-0s which was introduced by Fowler in 1911 and which could be found all over the system at this time. For a class which was not particularly highly regarded by many enginemen, it did come as something of a surprise that the LMS (successors to the Midland Railway) should construct a further 580 of these pleasant looking but (allegedly) not very efficient machines.

(*H. C. Casserley*)

STEAMING INTO BEDFORDSHIRE

The ten un-rebuilt Crosti 9F 2-10-0s (Nos. 92020-92029) were shedded at Wellingborough throughout their lives and were thoroughly hated by all who had to work on their footplates for the reason given on page 20. Not only that, the claimed savings in coal usage by preheating the water were outweighed by considerably increased maintenance costs, so it was not long before the preheat boilers were removed and all ten locomotives were rebuilt in conventional style and eventually dispersed, although they were always easily recognisable as ex-Crostis because they carried no smoke-deflectors.

BELOW Un-rebuilt No. 92022 is coasting gently past a permanent way gang in Leagrave station on its way to Brent with a coal train from Toton on Monday 23 April 1956. (*Harold Clements*)

Rebuilt Crosti No. 92020 slowly negotiates the up slow line through the northern suburbs of Luton with a lengthy ballast train on Thursday 18 October 1962. It is interesting to note the differences in the two locomotives (opposite and above) before and after rebuilding.

(*S. Summerson*)

In 1936, Luton Midland Road station buildings and platforms were modernised by being rebuilt into those with which we are familiar today. Light, airy and clinical, they presented a very up-to-date image of the LMS to the travelling public, and have remained largely unaltered ever since. Even so, in common with most other stations south of Bedford, there were only three platforms here at the time (no up slow) and it was not until the end of 1959 that this extra facility was added. Much double-heading was still taking place at this time as the service had been accelerated following the introduction of diesels, so it is very pleasant to see a single-headed train pulling in on the up fast for the stop on Saturday 30 April 1960. The locomotive is Jubilee 4-6-0 No. 45725 "Repulse" of Millhouses shed, Sheffield.

(*S. Summerson*)

Fairburn 2-6-4T No. 42159 of St Albans shed brings a long train of empty coaches from Cricklewood carriage sidings and eases it into Platform 3 of Luton Midland Road station on Wednesday 17 June 1959. Platform 4 (the up slow platform) to the left had yet to be built at the time, but it was not long in coming and opened on 9 November that same year to cater for the new diesel rail cars. (*S. Summerson*)

STEAMING INTO BEDFORDSHIRE

The southern end of Luton Midland Road station was as attractive a location to watch the trains in the steam era as anywhere in Bedfordshire, and the photographs on these two pages show why perfectly. Viewed together, they give an evocative picture of Luton as it was when they were taken during the afternoon of Saturday 11 March 1961. Today, about the only thing that remains unchanged is the hill in the background as virtually everything else – buildings, semaphore signals, telegraph poles, signal box, and, of course, the locomotive and train – has gone.

BELOW Royal Scot class 4-6-0 No. 46122 "Royal Ulster Rifleman", lately of Bushbury shed, rattles the nearby windows as it sits in Platform 2, waiting impatiently for the off with a train for St Pancras.

(*S. Summerson*)

Another Royal Scot, Kentish Town's No. 46142 "The York and Lancaster Regiment" shows perfect combustion as it cautiously approaches Platform 1 with a train from St Pancras. Surely no two pictures (opposite and above) could show more clearly what was lost to the railway world when modernisation encroached shortly after they were taken.

(*S. Summerson*)

STEAMING INTO BEDFORDSHIRE

Chiltern Green was the next station south of Luton up the Midland Main Line, and was called just that when it first opened to passenger trains in July 1868 – Chiltern Green. However, in a move no doubt intended to attract visitors to the nearby stately home, it underwent a 'makeover' at the end of 1891 and thereafter became Chiltern Green For Luton Hoo, a title it retained until closure to passenger trains in April 1952. Somewhat surprisingly perhaps, goods facilities were retained for another 15 years to cater primarily for the loading of new cars from the Vauxhall plant in Luton, but in March 1967 this amenity was withdrawn too, and all that remains today is the original station building standing back a little from the down fast line. Now it has become a private residence, and passengers speeding past in the comfort of their diesel or electric trains will be forgiven if they do not even notice it, nor realise that a station and goods yard existed here for a hundred years. There were platforms only on the 'main' and the goods sidings were to the east when the great photographer and prolific author Henry Casserley visited Chiltern Green with his camera on Thursday 13 July 1939 (he was one of only a handful so to do) to record the scenes shown on this page.

ABOVE Jubilee 4-6-0 No. 5644 "Howe" (carrying a Carlisle Kingmoor shed-plate) heads northwards under clear signals with an express goods train, but does not seem to be in too much of a hurry and has steam to spare on this windy pre-war summer's day.
(*H. C. Casserley*)

LEFT 4F 0-6-0 No. 4082 of St Albans shed occupies the up slow line with a short mixed-goods train and there is an unidentified 'Jocko' 0-6-0T (partly obscured) in the siding behind. (*H. C. Casserley*)

Harpenden station opened to passenger traffic in July 1868 and is now the only station between Luton and St Albans. Altered to Harpenden (Central) in 1950, it retained this title until 1966 when officially the 'Central' was dropped and it reverted to plain Harpenden, following closure of the ex-GN station Harpenden (East) and the branch to Hatfield in 1965. Trains for the Hemel Hempstead branch (closed in 1947) also used this station, and the disused bay platform for Hemel can be seen on the left of this 1957 photograph. Compound 4-4-0 No. 41181 is the locomotive in charge of the train which is an afternoon stopper from St Pancras to Leicester and the date is Thursday 21 March. (S. Summerson)

THE SANDY FOOTBRIDGE

In steam days it seemed that there was always something happening at Sandy, and a favourite viewing spot was the footbridge which spanned the tracks a hundred yards or so north of the station. Generations of trainspotters and photographers used it because from here everything which passed was viewable, and viewable with ease. There is still a footbridge in the same position today, but viewing from it has been made difficult deliberately because of the electric wires just below. Trains travelling along the East Coast Main Line were probably the major attraction for most enthusiasts who used the bridge, but nonetheless interesting were trains on the Cambridge line, like this pre-war photograph of rebuilt Precursor (now George V) class 4-4-0 No. 5241 "Napoleon" taken on Saturday 25 May 1935. It had only eight months life left at the time it was photographed here and was withdrawn before the number could be 'adjusted' by the addition of 20000 to 25241; something which befell those members of the class which survived past 1936. Of equal interest are the private-owner wagons below, some of which have Luton on their sides, indicating perhaps that they will only be travelling up the ECML as far as Welwyn where they will then be taken along the Dunstable branch to Luton. They are stationary here, with the locomotive driver no doubt waiting impatiently for something with a higher priority to pass on the main line so that he can take his lowly coal train through the bottleneck at the station and be on his way.

(Les Hanson)

Travelling in the opposite direction but in almost the same position as "Napoleon" opposite, ex LNWR 'Super D' No. 48951 of Bletchley climbs up the 1 in 125 gradient out of Sandy on Wednesday 30 July 1952, and heads back towards Bedford and base with a nice healthy-looking train from Cambridge. Local enthusiasts referred to this much-loved 663-strong class of 0-8-0 goods engines as 'Duck 8s', and in their own way, the wheezing and clanking noises that they made were as distinctive as anything else on the railway at the time. Fortunately one has been preserved (No. 49395), but it is unlikely to be seen out on the main line and just as unlikely to be able to muster up such an attractive consist as that seen here.

(*Les Hanson*)

The footbridge is featured again in these two views of expresses on the East Coast Main Line and, above, it can be seen over the last coaches of the up 'West Riding' as the train speeds southwards under clear signals on Bank Holiday Monday 7 August 1961. The locomotive is Doncaster shed's A1 Peppercorn Pacific No. 60125 "Scottish Union" which was to be seen here regularly at this time and is shown again later in the day on page 36. Opposite, the footbridge was the platform for the photographer of another speedy A1, this one No. 60148 "Aboyeur" of Copley Hill depot at the head of the 15.40 train from King's Cross to Leeds and Bradford on the same date. The Cambridge lines are prominent in both photographs (above, they are to the right, and, opposite, they are seen above the train). The appearance of double-track in these photographs is somewhat misleading as there was only a single track from here to Bedford (passing places at stations excepted). The track nearest the ECML is the running track, and the other is a siding with buffer-stops just short of the road bridge.

(Both photographs *Michael Mensing*)

ABOVE The footbridge is the photographer's vantage point in both of these August Bank Holiday Monday 1961 photographs. The quite remarkable 'passing shot' is all the more so when it is realised that both trains are moving! Approaching the camera (above) is the A1 Pacific "Scottish Union" which is also featured on page 34 as it hurried towards London earlier in the day. Here it is again after being refreshed and replenished at Top Shed (King's Cross), returning to Leeds and Bradford and about to pass one of the earlier design of Pacifics: a Gresley A3 (originally A1), now disfigured so cruelly here by the imposition of German-type 'elephant's ears'. The addition of these smoke deflectors was to cure the phenomenon of smoke drifting into the eyes of the crew, and this was achieved successfully, but it did nothing to improve the appearance of these otherwise classically beautiful locomotives. This particular A3 is No. 60047 "Donovan" of Grantham shed and it is on an up express which is thought to have come from Newcastle.

OPPOSITE A3 Pacific No. 60065, "Knight of Thistle", also of Grantham, (and its train) has been held at the signals by the footbridge in order to allow another train to pass on the up fast line and now it is slowly approaching the station with the 13.21 stopper from Peterborough to King's Cross. The sight of trains held here was very common throughout the steam era and was caused by the fact that there was room for only a single pair of tracks through the station, but this bottleneck and another further south at Arlesey were eliminated at the time of electrification. At Sandy this was made simple by the closure of the branch so that a new up platform could be constructed where the old Cambridge line buildings once stood. The only major bottleneck remaining on the southern section of the ECML today is the Welwyn Viaduct, and ambitious plans have been laid to eliminate it by the addition of two further lines on a completely new viaduct, but the need for this is tempered somewhat by the existence of the Hertford loop which in effect parallels the line over the viaduct.

(Both photographs *Michael Mensing*)

A panned photograph is one way of demonstrating the speed of the subject of course, and here on this double page spread are four of the best, each of a different class of locomotive and all taken near the footbridge below the Sandy sand-hills on August Bank Holiday Monday 7 August 1961. Above, the Gresley A4 streamlined Pacific No. 60034 "Lord Faringdon" of Top Shed is with a train which originated in Aberdeen at 07.30 and which would be in King's Cross within an hour of being seen here. Originally numbered 4903 and named "Peregrine", it was the last of the class to be built (in June 1938) and almost the last to be withdrawn (in August 1966). *(Michael Mensing)*

Peppercorn A1 Pacific No. 60130 "Kestrel" is on another up express and is one more example of how the railways liked to recycle good ideas when they became redundant, rather than waste them altogether. "Kestrel" was the original name of the streamlined A4 Pacific No. 4485 (later 60026) when it was built in 1937, but it was soon renamed "Miles Beevor" and the "Kestrel" name was unused until, along with several other bird names ("Kittiwake", "Curlew", "Osprey", "Sea Eagle", "Peregrine", etc.), it was applied to a new Peppercorn Pacific. *(Michael Mensing)*

Here is Standard Britannia class Pacific No. 70041 "Sir John Moore", recently displaced from Norwich depot and now working out of Immingham. Showing signs of severe neglect, it can hardly be described as being 'well kept' and contrasts markedly with the other locomotives on these two pages. The train is the 16.12 express from King's Cross to Cleethorpes, but despite its external condition, No. 70041 seems to be completely steam-tight and going well with just a light 'feather' showing from the safety valve. It was no wonder that the 'Brits' were so highly regarded, and a criminal shame that none saw more than 17 years (many saw much less) of revenue-earning service. (*Michael Mensing*)

This photograph shows perfectly why the Gresley A3 Pacifics were thought of by many observers as amongst the most handsome steam locomotives ever built and it completes this quartet of different classes. Even the later modification of a double chimney and a 'banjo' dome (as seen here) did nothing to diminish Sir Nigel Gresley's inspired outline. The example illustrated is No. 60108 "Gay Crusader" which is on the 16.05 express from King's Cross to Leeds and Bradford. "Gay Crusader" was one of the earliest of the class to be built as it emerged from Doncaster works in June 1923, just four months after the only A3 to be preserved: the ever popular No. 4472 (or 60103) "Flying Scotsman", which can still be seen well into the twenty-first century, occasionally passing this very spot at the head of an enthusiasts' special. (*Michael Mensing*)

The later class of A2 Pacifics (not to be confused with the Raven Pacifics which had all been withdrawn by 1937) was in reality four different classes, designated A2, A2/1, A2/2 and A2/3, the 40 members of which occupied the number sequence 60500 to 60539. Six (Nos. 60501-60506) were Thompson rebuilds of Gresleys P2 2-8-2s and designated A2/2, four (Nos. 60507-60510) which were originally meant to be V2 2-6-2s came out as A2/1 Thompson Pacifics, and 15 (Nos. 60500 and 60511-60524) were Thompson's own A2 Pacifics, but were reclassified A2/3 following his retirement. Finally, Peppercorn designed his own A2s, 15 of which were built (Nos. 60525-60539) from 1947. No. 60532 "Blue Peter" of this final batch is the only one to have survived into preservation. No. 60516 "Hycilla" of York shed (above) is a Thompson A2/3 and was photographed storming through Sandy on August Bank Holiday Monday 1961 at the head of the 12.20 train from Hull to King's Cross. *(Michael Mensing)*

The Gresley V2 class 2-6-2s have already been mentioned, without being illustrated, so here is a photograph of one of these particularly handsome machines (No. 60875 of Doncaster shed) leaving Sandy with a down parcels train on August Bank Holiday Monday 1961. Introduced by Gresley in 1936, this mixed traffic class was an immediate success and 184 were built, although the class leader was one of only eight to be named, and is preserved. It is No. 60800 "Green Arrow" which sometimes runs as No. 4771, and not surprisingly members of the class are referred to as "Green Arrows" as often as V2s. (*Michael Mensing*)

Gresley's streamlined A4 Pacifics caused a sensation when they first appeared in 1935 and have held a special place in the hearts of the British public, ever since "Mallard's" record-breaking dash down Stoke Bank in 1938 achieved an authenticated world speed record for steam traction of just over 126 mph. The chime whistles with which the 35 members of the class were fitted were instantly recognisable by enthusiasts and non-enthusiasts alike, and, when a chime was heard in the distance, there was often a quickening of the pulse at the thought of the impending sight of one of these undeniably magical machines in full flight. No wonder, therefore, that four have been preserved in this country whilst a further two are on display across the Atlantic. Top Shed's No. 60029 "Woodcock" (in the minority in the class in that it was never renamed!) has just passed under the line to Bedford as it speeds southwards with a relief express on August Bank Holiday Monday 1961. Some spans from this comparatively new structure were used when the station road bridge had to be raised at the time of electrification, so travellers are still able to cross (most of) it today, even though it has moved south by something like a quarter of a mile.

(*Michael Mensing*)

It is still possible to stand on the bridge from which this photograph and the one opposite were taken, although at the time it was open to road traffic, something which was banned a few years ago when barriers were erected to prevent anything much larger than a pedal cycle from passing across. A good view from here remains, although photographers generally prefer not to point their cameras through the overhead electric wires.

There was obviously no such impediment on August Bank Holiday Monday 1961 when this photograph of V2 No. 60897 was taken as it got under way again from the stop in the station. The train is the 16.21 stopper from King's Cross to Peterborough and the locomotive is yet another example of Top Shed's stock that was out and about on the ECML that day.
(*Michael Mensing*)

The first locomotive featured in this chapter is a 1906-built Precursor which became a George V on rebuilding in the early 1920s and here is another, although the one shown here was somewhat longer lived than "Napoleon". It is No. 25245 "Antæus" and is seen above coasting down the 1 in 125 slope for the stop in the station with a passenger train from Bletchley. The first of the Precursors was introduced in 1904 near the beginning of George Whale's six year tenure as Chief Mechanical Engineer of the LNWR and the last of the class were not withdrawn until the late 1940s when they had come through LMS influence and were then under the jurisdiction of British Railways. Much rebuilding had taken place under different Chief Mechanical Engineers and, although most members of the class retained the round-topped type of boiler, a few had been given Belpaire fireboxes, as was No. 25245, a locomotive which lasted until March 1941 before it was withdrawn for scrap. The date of this photograph is Saturday 1 May 1937.

(*Les Hanson*)

With shadows lengthening as the sun drops, the full beauty of Peppercorn A1 Pacific No. 60157 "Great Eastern" is highlighted as it takes a train of very mixed coaching-stock northwards through Sandy on Wednesday 30 July 1952. Enthusiasts have long felt the loss of the A1s as none was preserved. This loss was realised to be so great that for some years and against great odds, a dedicated group in Darlington has been constructing a totally new A1 from the original plans, so it may well be possible to recreate a scene such as this in the not too distant future, although the authorities would no doubt insist that the train be made up of very different vehicles from these!   (Les Hanson)

BLETCHLEY

The photographs on these two pages were taken of trains in exactly the same spot six years apart, but although seen from different angles, nothing much (other than the locomotives) seems to have changed. Even the wooden post supporting the home signal on the left has survived unaltered, but it would not be too long before the whole place was to change beyond all recognition.

Bletchley's own Standard Class 4 4-6-0 No. 75036 is waiting to take an evening train to Oxford on Saturday 3 August 1957.   (*S. Summerson*)

Midland 3P 4-4-0 No. 40743 of Bedford shed awaits the off with the 09.30 train to Oxford on Monday 23 July 1951. Passengers who travelled from Bedford (or indeed from anywhere along the line from Bedford) were often nonplussed the first time they took this train as it was advertised as a through service yet they were turfed out on arrival in the Bedford platform and told to cross the footbridge to the Oxford platform where (eventually) they were able, if lucky, to return to the same seat on the same train, often to be hauled the rest of the way by the same locomotive! To comply with some obscure regulation or other, the train had to cross all four tracks of the WCML empty, and then set back into the platform shown here. Just to compound matters, trains running in the opposite direction from Oxford were allowed to run straight into the Bedford platform! To the travelling public such antics were totally incomprehensible, and it was never made clear to them why in the case illustrated here it was impossible for the train to continue on to Oxford from the platform into which it had run from Bedford.

(*H. C. Casserley*)

STEAMING INTO BEDFORDSHIRE

The Bletchley flyover was under construction during much of 1959, but right from the outset it was usually referred to by locals and enthusiasts alike as the 'White Elephant'. Built in conjunction with a proposed enlargement to the marshalling-yard at Swanbourne (which never materialised), the new flyover carried very little traffic, and although it facilitated movement of trains between the up side and the down side of the WCML, there were never all that many which needed to carry out such a manoeuvre anyway! But it did see some use, and here are two photographs to prove it.

Standard Class 4 4-6-0 No. 75038 is climbing up from the northern end with a parcels train on Thursday 30 July 1964, and opposite, Black Five 4-6-0 No. 44869 is travelling the other way, also with a parcels train, on Tuesday 27 October of the same year. In the above photograph the railway staff's cars, including a Morris Minor and a Ford Anglia are parked beneath, and although the gantries are up, there is no sign yet of the overhead wiring, nor of the insulators, nor any of the other paraphernalia associated with overhead high voltage wiring – in this case 25kV. *(C. Stacey)*

The contractors can be seen to have been busy since the photograph opposite was taken, as the wires have now appeared, along with all the necessary bits and pieces; this having been completed in just three months. For many years, steam locomotives were banned from running under energised wires in the erroneous belief that their exhaust might cause a flashover, but it eventually came to be realised that this would not happen, and once again Bletchley sees the occasional steam special passing under the wires and under the flyover. "Duke of Gloucester", "Flying Scotsman" and double-headed Standard 2-6-4Ts (to mention just some) have all been through Bletchley in recent times, and when in happens, there is a definite sense of déjà vu amongst those viewers who are old enough to remember the real thing. 'Its not quite the same', you might hear some of them say, but in the absence of anything better, it'll do for now! (*C. Stacey*)

In the summer of 1959 when this photograph was taken, there was still no visible sign of the impending decimation of Bletchley's railway infrastructure. Signal boxes were still intact and operative, tall semaphore signals dominated this (the north) end of the station and water columns were maintained in working order in case a steam locomotive took but a short measure as it passed over the troughs. Sidings were full and there was a general feeling of high activity about the place at almost any hour. Enormously long trains still stopped, and it was common practice to see 16 coaches or more (as here) behind a single locomotive. Double-heading was not unknown on this part of the WCML in steam days, but was definitely the exception rather than the rule (unlike the Midland where the reverse was the case), and on this page, Royal Scot class 4-6-0 No. 46122 "Royal Ulster Rifleman" of Bushbury shed is seen coasting in for the stop with a typically lengthy train (probably from Holyhead) for Euston. *(David Eatwell)*

It was all go at Bletchley during much of 1959 and the importance of the junction station was being maintained by the construction of the flyover which would allow trains on the Oxford-Cambridge line to cross the WCML without having to wait for a clear path. Not that there were all that many trains which actually travelled on the cross-country route at the time, but perhaps it was hoped that this traffic would increase dramatically and justify the enormous expense involved. Soon after it opened, much of the line from Bletchley to Oxford fell into disuse, but fortunately it was never ripped up and there is currently talk of it being reopened right the way through as part of the 'new' East-West route, in which case the flyover may very well come into its own at last.

On a misty day (Saturday 30 May 1959) work can be seen to be in full swing on the great White Elephant (the new flyover) as Willesden's Black Five 4-6-0 No. 45064 restarts a stopping train for Euston out of the up slow platform. In a scene full of interest, note particularly the 'abandoned' trolley on the right, the 'WET PAINT' sign in front of the seat, the unattended mail-bag (surely not containing First Class Post!) just lying on the platform and (to the right of the furthest lamp-post) the 'C' sign, indicating the start of the speed-restriction (for the flyover construction) ahead. If only today's railways had half as much fascination.

(*H. C. Casserley*)

Just after the end of World War II, enough passengers wanted to travel from Watford to Bletchley early in the morning for there to be a regular train to take them, and here it is: the 06.24 Watford to Bletchley local, just after arrival on Saturday 3 July 1948. It is pure speculation of course, but it may very well be that the photographer, who lived adjacent to the WCML, had just alighted from this very train in order to capture on film the wartime (1942) rebuilt Jubilee class 4-6-0 locomotive No. 45735 "Comet" of Camden shed, still running without the smoke deflectors which it was soon to gain. Just two Jubilees were rebuilt with more efficient boilers (No. 45736 "Phoenix" was the other) and so successful were these Stanier rebuilds that they formed the basis of the rebuilt Royal Scot class which had come out under Fowler in 1927 and now were starting to show their age. No more Jubilees were to be rebuilt, but all 71 members of the Royal Scot class were, as were 18 of the 52 Patriots. The rebuilding programme was a slow and lengthy process, and it was not until December 1954 that the last Royal Scot class locomotive was eventually dealt with. This was No. 46137 "The Prince of Wales's Volunteers South Lancashire" which ironically lasted only another nine years before it went to the scrap yard, a move which hardly made sound economic sense. (*H. C. Casserley*)

The Precursor 4-4-0s were introduced in 1904 and have already been shown on branch line work in the 'Sandy Footbridge' chapter, but here is another (also a rebuild) on the West Coast Main Line, although this one would appear to be about to leave Bletchley's down slow platform and is thus most likely to be on a stopping train for Northampton, perhaps, or Rugby. No. 25319 "Bucephalus" was photographed near the end of its illustrious career on Saturday 25 June 1938, just 20 months before withdrawal.

(Les Hanson)

The beautifully proportioned 4-6-0s of the Prince of Wales class were introduced in 1911 under Bowen-Cooke and production continued almost until the time of the amalgamation in 1923 when the LNWR became part of the newly formed LMS. Various members of the class could be seen with either round-topped or Belpaire boilers and it was not uncommon for any one locomotive to start out in life with a round topped boiler, to come out of the works after a refit with a Belpaire and to revert to round-topped again some time later, all of which kept the rivet-counting fraternity of the day deliriously happy.

Built in 1915, "Livingstone" (above) was renumbered No. 5664 by the LMS in 1927 and painted red, a colour which had almost become the private property of the Midland Railway until the creation of the Big Four.

Across the platform and in front of "Livingstone" is Precursor 4-4-0 No. 5242 "Ionic" of 1906, on shed, and both are seen at the northern end of Bletchley station some time during the 1930s.   (*S. Summerson collection*)

Of the same class as No. 5664 opposite, No. 25798 was photographed wearing express headlights whilst on stand-by duty at the north end of Bletchley station on Saturday 21 May 1938, and was initially withdrawn from service only three months later that August, but because of the war it was reinstated in 1940. Happily, this new lease of life was to last another five years, but final withdrawal coincided with the end of hostilities in Europe, and No. 25798 made its final journey when it went to the scrap yard in June 1945.

(Les Hanson)

STEAMING INTO BEDFORDSHIRE

One of the least glamorous jobs for a locomotive around a busy station was that of station pilot, although the busiest stations of all would need more than one to keep the platform roads clear and ready for use. There was never a hard and fast rule about which classes should be used, although at some stations there was actually a designated locomotive, such as the beautifully turned out little J72 0-6-0T No. 68736 which ran in NER green at Newcastle-on-Tyne as late as the early 1960s. At Bletchley it was common for a 0-6-0T 'Jocko' (*never* called a 'Jinty' in this part of the world!) to be seen performing this mundane duty.

On Wednesday 5 May 1965 the station pilot job fell to locally-shedded No. 47521, seen (above) with a horse-box in the up fast platform at the northern end of the station, a position it would not be able to maintain for very much longer as another London-bound express would be sure to come along shortly and would not take too kindly to finding its way blocked by the little 'Jocko'.

(*Ken Fairey*)

Stanier's Coronation class Pacifics had been seen at Bletchley since their introduction in 1937, and many was the time one would stop on its way to Euston or the north. However, when this photograph was taken in 1964 their reign was almost over, and they were about to abdicate in favour of the soon-to-be-introduced new breed of English Electric diesels. Bletchley's importance was soon to decline in favour of nearby Milton Keynes and trains would stop there instead. It was all very sad as Willesden shed's No. 46240 "City of Coventry" (see also page 116) pulled away after a stop on Thursday 4 June and was about to pass under the flyover on its way to Euston, not quite for the last time, but very nearly.

(*Ken Fairey*)

With a fair degree of determination on display, station pilot 'Jocko' No. 47521 is seen (above) as it purposefully approaches the platforms at the north end of the station on Tuesday 13 October 1964. A member of a class not really noted for its speed, the 0-6-0T obviously has an important mission to accomplish, and by the looks of things it will soon be there to do it. By this date, electrification is starting to encroach as can be seen by the appearance of the overhead gantries, and before long the 'Jockos' will all be gone. Diesel shunters will then be employed in their stead; more efficient no doubt but nothing like so entertaining. (*C. Stacey*)

The first railway in Bedfordshire was the Bedford Railway which connected the county town with Bletchley and which began business on 17 November 1846. By then the LNWR was becoming well established, and Bedfordians wishing to travel to London were exhorted to use this somewhat indirect route because at the time there was no other (see poster on page 130). Push-pull trains operated along the route during much of the 1930s, '40s and '50s, and members of this class of small tank engines (built by the Midland Railway between 1881 and 1900) were often to be seen working them just as No. 1295 was on Saturday 10 April 1948. The smart little 0-4-4T has just arrived with the 10.20 train from Bedford and has set back to take water at the column at the north end of the station.

(H. C. Casserley)

STATIONS
Wellingborough Midland Road

Situated just 65 miles north of St Pancras on the Midland Main Line, Wellingborough was a really busy place in steam days, and there seemed always to be some activity at the town's principal station. The other was Wellingborough London Road, and this was on the cross country line between Northampton and Peterborough. It is shown on pages 76 and 77. As well as catering for main line trains, Wellingborough Midland Road was near the junction with the short line to Higham Ferrers, and on Friday 22 March 1959 Standard class 2 2-6-2T No. 84008 is shown as it was about to leave with the 13.00 train up the branch. No. 84008 was built at Crewe in 1953 and ended its working life just 12 years later at Leicester from where it was withdrawn in October 1965.   (*Ken Fairey*)

Bedford Midland Road

Bedford also had (but in this case has retained) more than one station. Midland Road catered for main line passengers, as well as those taking a branch train to Northampton or Hitchin. St John's is the second station which at one time facilitated travel to Sandy and Cambridge in the easterly direction and Bletchley and Oxford to the west. The original St John's has virtually vanished and a halt with the name St John's has been opened nearby following the sensible diversion of Bletchley trains into Bedford Midland Road. Before the London extension opened in 1867/8, passengers on the Midland Main Line (as it was then) travelled to the capital via Shefford to Hitchin where they joined the Great Northern and continued southwards with the begrudging permission of that rival company. When the St Pancras route via Luton opened, the Hitchin line became but a humble branch line which was eventually singled over much of its length, and remained thus until closure in 1962. Bedford Midland Road retained a Hitchin bay for trains on this route and on Sunday 24 June 1961 the last member of the Ivatt Class 2 2-6-2Ts, Bedford's auto-fitted No. 41329, impatiently awaits departure in the late afternoon sunshine. (*MNLPS*)

Leagrave

Leagrave station is barely two miles down the line from Luton and yet has always been a comparatively busy place, a feature still noticeable today as it serves the large population in and near the south of the county's biggest town. Not noticeable at all today though are milk churns waiting on a platform as all milk business was purloined by road tankers long since. In steam days Leagrave had extensive sidings, and these saw much coming and going, mainly of coal wagons. No up slow platform existed here until the introduction of accelerated services with the influx of diesel traction in 1959, and 3Fs or 4Fs were a common sight shunting in the adjacent yard.

Not so common was the sight of a Horwich mogul 2-6-0, and No. 42771, shown in this photograph, spent some time shunting at Leagrave on this date (see also page 139). On the up fast line is one of the few Stanier Jubilee class 4-6-0s to carry a straight-sided tender along here at this time and is No. 45568 "Western Australia" taking an express to St Pancras on Monday 20 April 1953. Today's footbridge spans all four tracks and occupies a position slightly to the north of the one depicted here. A short siding is all that is left of the goods yard today. (*Harold Clements*)

Leagrave

The passage of an express fitted goods train on the down fast line through Leagrave station goes unnoticed by virtually everyone except the photographer on the fine sunny afternoon of Monday 19 September 1955. The siding on the left is as heavily occupied as ever, and the whole scene features much interesting railway 'furniture'. The signal box stands clear under the footbridge, lamps hanging beneath delicately curved supports adorn lamp-posts on both platforms, Midland Railway fencing marks the station boundary on the right and access to the trains is achieved through the solid-looking station building which survives to this day. The speeding train is being hauled by Standard Class 5 4-6-0 No. 73065 which is a member of a class introduced in 1951 and which was very obviously based on Stanier's Black Fives of 1934. Even after nationalisation, it seemed the LMS ruled, OK? *(Harold Clements)*

Luton

Just as Wellingborough and Bedford had two stations, so too had Luton, and although the ex-GNR Bute Street station closed to passengers in 1965, Luton obviously saw itself as more than a single station town, so it was justifiably proud when once again it reverted to two-station importance with the opening of Luton Airport Parkway in 1999. The Midland Railway's Luton station is just over 30 miles out of St Pancras and came into use for passengers in July 1868. It was renamed Luton Midland Road in September 1950 and reverted to Luton soon after Bute Street closed. Much development took place on the site over the years and in 1936 the old station was completely rebuilt and modernised. The atmospheric

photographs on these two pages show it as it was in LMS days, prior to that rebuilding. Above, the view is to the north with the up and down goods lines shown in the foreground, beyond which is a terminating bay platform and Luton North signal box prominent in the centre. The area has been substantially modified since, first for the new diesel service in the late 1950s, then again in the late 1970s to accommodate the expanded electric services. The goods sidings, together with the associated buildings, have been swept away to provide more space for car parking, necessitated by the deserved popularity of today's greatly enhanced train service.

(F. C. Clements)

Luton

A deserted view of Luton station looking south. Another delightfully peaceful scene which this time is dominated by a very tall MR lower quadrant semaphore signal. However, the tranquillity is about to be disturbed as a train is signalled on the down goods line. As with the north end of Luton station, extensive remodelling has taken place with the three platforms in view now expanded to five and the goods lines upgraded into passenger-carrying slow lines.

(*F. C. Clements*)

Letchworth

Various schemes to connect Oxford with Cambridge were put forward during the early spread of the railways, and in 1845 one such would have taken the 73-mile line through Luton and Royston, but so stormy was the Act's passage through Parliament that in the event only the section that headed north-eastwards from Hitchin to Great Shelford (south of Cambridge on the Eastern Counties Railway as it was then) was built. As we now know, the eventual route was 77 miles long and went via Bletchley, Bedford and Sandy, but high hopes for the Luton route were expressed at the time and a crossing of the London & Birmingham Railway at Cheddington was proposed. But it was not to be, and a line through Letchworth eventually opened in 1850, although it was not until 1905 that the town was given its first 'station' which is the first one out of Hitchin. It was originally but a humble halt which consisted of little more than wooden platforms, but in 1913 the GNR replaced it with a 'permanent' station more befitting Letchworth's status as the world's first garden city. So highly did the GNR then regard the population of Letchworth that, as well as providing a stylish and substantial building for them, the new facilities included a feature normally provided only at the most important of stations, i.e. a lift to transport passengers between street level and the platforms down below. Today, name-boards have been changed to proclaim 'Letchworth Garden City', and it is most appropriate that the building enjoys 'Listed Grade 2' status.   (*North Hertfordshire Museums*)

Letchworth

Two more old postcards of Letchworth are shown here (both undated), and this time they depict the station at rail level.

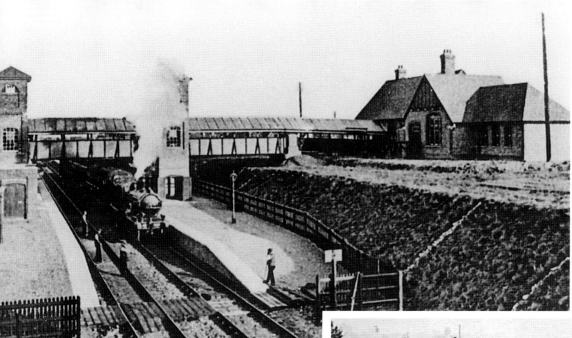

LEFT The back of the building shown opposite is clearly recognisable with the tower above the lift-shaft prominent on the left and an early Ivatt locomotive standing at the platform with a train for Hitchin. Members of the permanent way gang are showing due respect for the train as they take a break from their labours and lean on their shovels for a moment as they stand clear to await the departure of the train before they resume work around the barrow-crossing at the end of the platform.

(*North Hertfordshire Museums*)

RIGHT No. 209 has just arrived at Letchworth round about the year 1910, probably with an excursion which is heading in the Cambridge direction. The date can be presumed to be fairly accurate as this is the original Letchworth station which opened in April 1905 and which was replaced in May 1913 with the listed building which survives to this day. No. 208 is an Ivatt 2-4-0 which was built in May 1881 and which was withdrawn in December 1913. The crowds on the platforms suggest that holiday outings are the order of the day, yet not a lot of interest is being shown in this particular train.

(*North Hertfordshire Museums*)

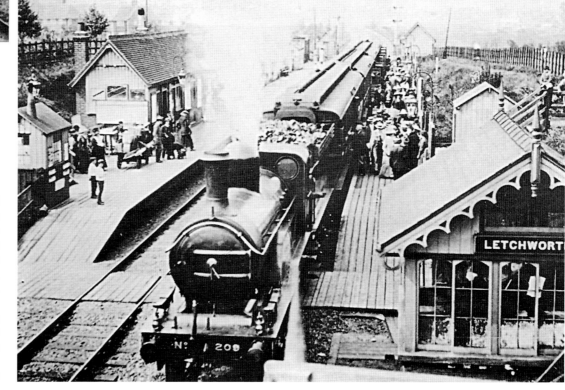

Dunstable

Dunstable Town station was known as Church Street prior to renaming in 1927 and saw its last passengers in April 1965 with through goods traffic due to cease some nine months later.

LEFT An undated old postcard, thought to be from the 1890s, shows a train for Luton pulling away below Blows Downs whilst station staff pose self-consciously for the camera. (*Bryan Cross collection*)

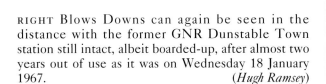

RIGHT Blows Downs can again be seen in the distance with the former GNR Dunstable Town station still intact, albeit boarded-up, after almost two years out of use as it was on Wednesday 18 January 1967. (*Hugh Ramsey*)

Luton Bute Street

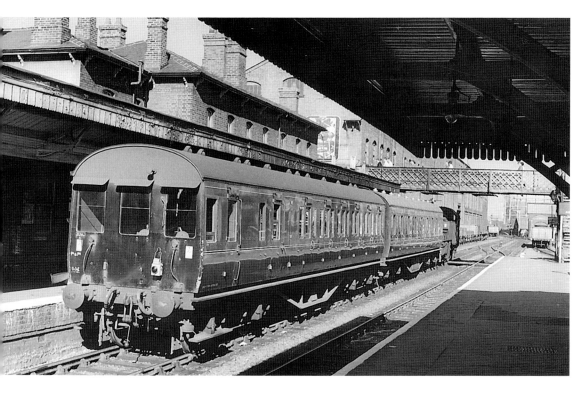

One of the rare through push-and-pull workings from Leighton Buzzard is seen at Luton Bute Street forming the return 08.30 working on Friday 8 June 1962, just a month before this service ceased. The original GNR service to Hatfield (in the opposite direction) lasted somewhat longer and was not withdrawn until April 1965. Prior to the official closure in 1991 (when the track was severed in Luton to allow expansion of the car park), the single line remained in use for the conveyance of cement (ceased 1988) and oil (ceased 1989) to terminals sited just short of the town's other station: the ex-LNWR/LMS Dunstable North. Since then, numerous proposals have been made for the route including steam driving courses, a tram-link, an express bus-way and modernisation (including electrification) for it to become part of the Thameslink national network, but none of these has reached fruition. At one time a preservation group had plans to run their own trains along part of the route, but 'authority' soon scuppered this imaginative (and potentially popular) scheme by having vital sections of the remaining track removed. In this photograph, the driver's cab in the auto trailer can be clearly examined whilst at the opposite end Ivatt 2P 2-6-2T No. 41289 provides the motive power. Seen just beyond the footbridge, the old GNR goods warehouse saw final use as a progress centre for staff on the Midland electrics to learn all about Customer Care. *(S. Summerson)*

Table 16.—Luton and Dunstable Branch. (Junction with the Main Line at Leighton.)

London & North Western Railway timetable of September 1878. (Note: Stanbridgeford incorrectly listed as Stanbridge Ford.)

Woburn Sands

On an unspecified date, thought to be in the late 1950s, Stanier 2-6-4T No. 42573 draws into Woburn Sands with an up local train heading towards Bletchley. The level crossing gates are still operated at this time by the huge wheel which dominates the end of the small signal box and a Mk 1 Ford Cortina awaits the opening of the gates. Today, these have been replaced by barriers which are operated from inside the same signal box, and this may well be the thin end of the wedge as sweeping proposals to upgrade the whole line have been made which, if implemented, will undoubtedly see the end of this charmingly old fashioned branch line as we have known it (and loved it) for so long. (*John Spencer*)

Bedford St John's

On Saturday 3 August 1957, Ivatt 2P 2-6-2T No. 41222 of Bletchley shed is stabled in the centre road at Bedford St John's station between trips to and from its home base. This was Bedford's first railway station (it opened in 1846) but today the site is heavily overgrown and is something of an eyesore following the demolition of buildings and the diversion of services into Bedford Midland in 1984. It is still possible to find the platform edges with perseverance, but nothing else of railway interest remains at this once very important location. However, hope of a possible renaissance is evident following proposals for the re-establishment of the East-West link, so track could once again be laid through the old station site and trains could once again be travelling this way between Oxford and Cambridge. Well, maybe!

(*S. Summerson*)

Bedford St John's

Built at Swindon in 1953 and delivered new to Bletchley depot, BR Standard Class 4 4-6-0 No. 75038 drifts through Bedford St John's station and passes the water tank as it heads back towards its home depot. Behind the Standard's BR2 tender, an 8F 2-8-0 can just be seen setting back past a ground signal. No. 75038 had a short working life of but twelve years during which it was allocated to just two depots. Soon after this photograph was taken in 1964 it moved to Shrewsbury, and it was from there that it was withdrawn in 1965. On the left can be seen the van used daily to transport parcels between here and Midland Road, at this time steam-hauled, but latterly a turn for a diesel shunter.

(*Ian Hall*)

Bedford St John's

Bedford stalwart 2P 2-6-2T No. 41329 (the last of the class) shunts its stock prior to departing from St John's station with the 11.10 train for Bletchley on Saturday 19 March 1955. Following demotion to unstaffed status, the up platform, together with a small portion of the overall shelter, remained in use until the replacement St John's station came into use in 1984 (see page 104). Pedestrian access to the new station is via steps down from Ampthill Road Bridge whilst the nearest car park is part of what was the site of the Cox & Danks scrapyard off Melbourne Street (see page 97).

(*R. J. Buckley*)

Harpenden Central

Harpenden is yet another of those towns which once sported the luxury of two stations, but Harpenden East went out of use in April 1965 when the ex-GN line between Hatfield and Luton closed, and Harpenden station (which had been known as Harpenden Central since September 1950) resumed sole responsibility for the town's rail-travelling public. Harpenden, at almost 25 miles from St Pancras, was also the junction station for the Hemel Hempstead branch which saw its last passenger train in June 1947, although the old bay platform was still to be seen in later years. On Saturday 1 June 1957, pristine Black Five 4-6-0 No. 44812 of Kentish Town shed was photographed at Harpenden Central at the head of a local service to St Pancras. The first four vehicles of the train are passenger coaches and behind them is a selection of parcel vehicles.

(*S. Summerson*)

Harpenden Central

On the same date as the photograph opposite, Kentish Town's Stanier Class 3 2-6-2T No. 40160 sits shorn of headlamps at the front of a terminating passenger train from St Pancras in the down slow platform of Harpenden Central station with the driver looking towards the rear as if waiting for instructions. With these clues in mind, it is perhaps not unreasonable to surmise that a shunting movement might be about to take place, and once the carriage doors have been closed, the train will vacate this spot to allow the passage of trains heading for Luton, Bedford and the north. (*S. Summerson*)

Wellingborough London Road

Wellingborough London Road station was on the LNWR cross country line which ran between Northampton and Peterborough and thus provided a connection with the Midland Main Line. The last five miles of the route survived the destruction which befell the remainder of the line and is today one of England's premier preserved lines: the Nene Valley Railway which operates out of Wansford on the Great North Road. The whole of the London Road site was cleared after the line closed and is now part of the A45 trunk road, but the station building was quite magnificent for such a minor station and its destruction was therefore something of a disaster. However, two other buildings of similar style along this same stretch of line have survived to be admired, and they are at Oundle (this is now a private residence on the western outskirts of town) and at Wansford station on the NVR. Above, on Friday 1 May 1964, Ivatt 2-6-2T No. 41225 is just departing London Road on the (short) last leg of its journey from Northampton to Midland Road just four days before passenger services were withdrawn from the line. (*Ken Fairey*)

Wellingborough London Road

Some four years earlier than the picture opposite, on Saturday 28 May 1960, the train contained an extra coach and the motive power considerably more tractive effort! Black Five 4-6-0 No. 45324 was the locomotive in charge of the 16.45 service to Northampton on that date and the photographer's elevated position gives a splendid view of the whole location as the 4-6-0 coasts in for the stop. Amongst all the railwayana in the background, the junction signals for the spur to Wellingborough Midland Road can be seen quite clearly. *(Ken Fairey)*

Newport Pagnell

The four-mile long Wolverton to Newport Pagnell branch opened in 1867 and carried passengers through to 1964 when that service was withdrawn, although goods were still carried until final closure in 1967. There were two intermediate stations (Bradwell and Great Linford) which meant that, including the termini, there were four stations in four miles which surely must be some kind of record. Apparently it was intended originally that the branch should continue through to Olney (on the Bedford-Northampton line) and some earthworks were completed, but along with many similar schemes at the time, it foundered and was never completed. There is virtually no sign of the railway in Newport Pagnell now, although much of the trackbed between there and Wolverton has been turned into a footpath/cycle track firmly within the boundaries of Milton Keynes. On Saturday 14 June 1958, auto-fitted Ivatt 2-6-2T No. 41275 of Bletchley is allowed to release a little extra steam prior to departure as the two-man crew take a rest on the platform and share the daily paper before having to undergo the exertions of the return journey to Wolverton. (See also rear end-paper.)

(S. Summerson)

Luton Hoo and Flitwick

RIGHT It was on Thursday 25 October 1855 that the first sod was turned in the construction of what was then the Luton, Dunstable & Welwyn Railway, and it was on Monday 26 April 1965 that passenger services were withdrawn from the same line, by then usually referred to as the Hatfield, Luton & Dunstable Railway. But it was not just the railway which had a name-change as more than half the stations en route suffered the same fate in one form or another during their lives. The most drastic changes occurred to just two stations: Dunstable Church Street became Dunstable Town in 1927 (see page 68) and, most severe of all, New Mill End became Luton Hoo in 1891. Of course, there was a station on the nearby Midland Main Line with the words Luton Hoo in the title as Chiltern Green (see page 30) included the words 'For Luton Hoo' from the same year until closure, but whatever their titles, these two stations, located no more than half a mile apart across the valley, must have been used by fewer passengers than any other in the county. In the accompanying photograph of Luton Hoo station taken about 1923/24, the two passengers appear to be school children, but the angle of the shadows suggests that it is an afternoon view, so possibly they are waiting to return home after a day out somewhere nearby. Luton Hoo, perhaps?   (*F. C. Clements*)

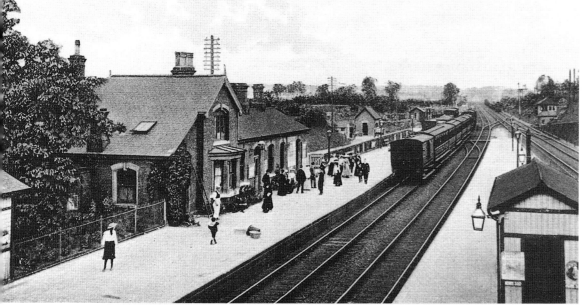

LEFT Flitwick station is 9½ miles south of Bedford and opened to passenger traffic on 2 May 1870. Following the closure of Ampthill in 1959, it is now the first stop for local trains on their way to London (or beyond) from Bedford and retained its charm throughout the whole of its existence until electrification (and thus modernisation) reared its ugly head in 1982/83. In this postcard, dated about 1905, the 'olde worlde' attraction is plain for all to see as a north-bound passenger train leaves the down fast platform whilst a goods train on the up slow approaches the station signal box. On the platform, 'best clothes' are evident, suggesting an event of some importance has taken (or is about to take) place.   (*David Eatwell collection*)

PORTRAITS

Webb's LNWR 0-6-2T 'Coal Tanks' were a much-loved and familiar class of workhorses, and some 300 of them were built between 1881 and 1896. So, here are two photographs of one that will be familiar to anyone who watched the trains on the Leighton Buzzard-Dunstable North branch in the 1940s and early 1950s. It was shedded at Bletchley during much of that period and happily hauled trains up and down Sewell Bank between the two towns with no complaints.

RIGHT It is seen at Leighton Buzzard, taking a rest at the head of a passenger train for Dunstable North on Wednesday 13 August 1952 with Driver Alec Kerr and Fireman Edward (Teddy) Wells posing proudly for the camera. (*Harold Clements*)

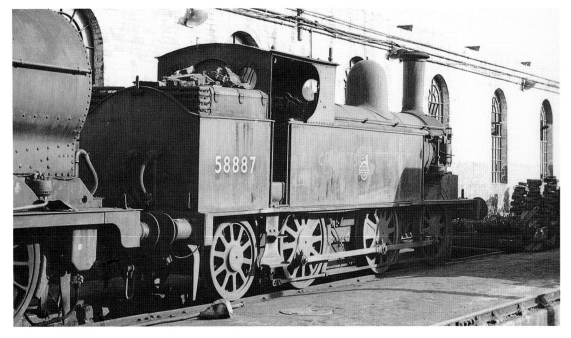

LEFT No. 58887 is taking an even longer rest beside Bletchley shed in September 1953, by now not being given a great deal to do to keep it occupied. A regular performer along the branch for many years, this particular locomotive was built in December 1881 and was given the number 252 by the LNWR. In September 1921 it became No. 3751 in the duplicate list and was given the number 7596 by the LMS. In April 1936 it was again renumbered, this time to 27596 and was first withdrawn in March 1939, only to be reinstated in 1940. Its BR number 58887, as carried here, was applied in June 1948, and final withdrawal came in April 1955. Fortunately, No. 58926 has been preserved in a beautiful black livery with the number 1054, and has even been entrusted with the haulage of special trains on the main line. (*S. Summerson collection*)

Another Webb design for the LNWR is shown here in the shape of his 5' 6" wheeled 2-4-2T class, 160 of which were built between 1890 and 1897. They had radial axles at both ends and were constructed specifically to carry larger quantities of coal and water than the earlier 2-4-0Ts and 2-4-2Ts. Many minor differences could be found throughout the class, including coal-rails on the bunker (some had them, others did not) and the side tanks (some had long ones and some had short), but whatever the differences were, there was no denying that Webb's '2-4-2 Tanks', as they were known, were extremely elegant and solid looking locomotives.

No. 6708 (above) is at work at Bletchley on Saturday 22 June 1935 and (below) No. 910 (later to become LMS 6601 and BR 46601) was shedded at Bletchley for many years. As No. 46601 it hauled the last train on the Aylesbury branch on Saturday 31 January 1953 and was scrapped the following December.   (ABOVE *John Dewing*, BELOW *Bryan Cross collection*)

STEAMING INTO BEDFORDSHIRE

Spot the differences. These are both Bowen-Cooke designed Prince of Wales class 4-6-0s, so named, as was often the case, after the first locomotive in the class. This appeared in 1912 and was in effect a lengthened version of the 4-4-0 George the Fifth class of locomotives. The two shown here were photographed at Bletchley on Saturday 25 June 1938.

No. 25763 (above) has a round-topped boiler, a straight running-plate and inside motion, whereas No. 25845 has a Belpaire boiler, an 'up-and-down' running-plate and outside valve gear. Five of the class had this unusual outside valve gear and were nicknamed 'Tishies', some say because of the 'strange' sounds they made while working. No. 25845 (left) was the last ever LNWR locomotive to be built but ironically it was chosen by the LMS to represent them at the 1924 Wembley Exhibition. It never carried an LNWR number and was given a red livery for the show, along with (temporarily) the name "Prince of Wales". No. 25763 was scrapped in November 1939, but 'Tishy' continued to work all through World War II and often travelled through Bedford on the Cambridge branch until its end came in September 1947.   (Both photographs *Les Hanson*)

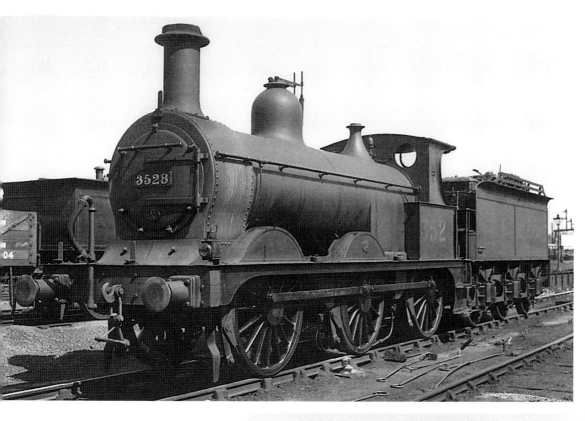

LEFT No. 3528 was a Johnson-designed, Neilson-built 0-6-0 of 1897 for the Midland Railway, and was photographed at Bedford on Saturday 22 June 1935. Known as the 'Johnson Goods', the whole class was built with round-topped boilers, but some were replaced later with the Belpaire type. These 2Fs lasted well, were sterling workers and the final ones were not withdrawn until January 1964. (*John Dewing*)

RIGHT No. 43785 is typical of the 3Fs that were widespread throughout the old LMS area and was one of a class of non-superheated 0-6-0s that was introduced in 1903. Despite their inferior tractive effort, they were generally preferred by enginemen to the much more numerous 4Fs, about which it was hard to find a good word being spoken. No. 43785 was photographed beside Bedford Junction signal box on Saturday 24 September 1955. (*H. C. Casserley*)

This photograph shows MR 2183 class 4-4-0 No. 2201 beside Bedford locomotive shed with members of the almost obligatory cleaning gang looking very proud and taking a well-earned rest from their labours. The class was built by Sharp Stewart of Glasgow from 1892, and as No. 2201 was the penultimate example to be delivered. It came here new in 1892, which is when it would appear to have been photographed. From 1907, locomotives of the class were renumbered in the series 403-407, and were extensively rebuilt under Deeley between 1914 and 1922 to become the 483 class. *(David Walker collection)*

Two more 4-4-0s are shown here which, as can be seen, are not only very different from the 4-4-0 opposite but are also very different from each other.

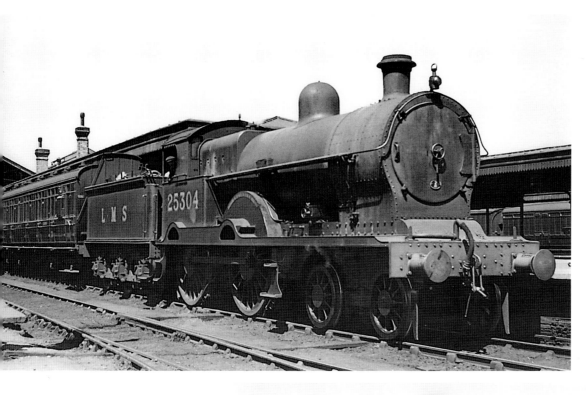

LEFT Rebuilt Precursor No. 25304 "Greyhound" is shown at Bletchley on Saturday 21 May 1938, about to leave for Oxford with a train of fine-looking clerestory coaches. The class was introduced by the LNWR in 1904, and "Greyhound's" original number was 302. In LMS ownership it became 5304 but that company eventually instigated a renumbering scheme and 5304 became 25304 in 1936. The Precursors began to be phased out in the late 1930s, and were succeeded on many duties by Prince of Wales 4-6-0s as locomotives of this class were themselves being replaced by the new Stanier designs. (*Les Hanson*)

RIGHT No. 750 is one of the original Johnson 3P class 4-4-0s which was introduced in 1901. This particular one dates from 1904 and was photographed near the shed at Bedford on Saturday 22 June 1935. Like the rest of the class, it was rebuilt under Fowler with a super-heater, but although many of its brothers lasted well into the post-war nationalisation period, No. 750 was not so lucky and made its acquaintance with the breaker's torch in 1939. (*John Dewing*)

The Jones Goods No. 103 was the first of a class of 15 locomotives which were built for the Highland Railway in 1894 and thus became the first 4-6-0 in Britain. Upon official withdrawal during the 1930s, it was decided to preserve this historically important locomotive and it was put on display wearing the Highland Railway's green livery. However, No. 103 underwent restoration to full working order in 1959 when it was repainted in Stroudly yellow (a livery used by the HR towards the end of the nineteenth century) and worked a very successful series of enthusiasts' specials, mainly in Scotland. Just why it was chosen to masquerade as a French locomotive in a British period comedy film we may never know, but chosen it was and the film makers had to use all their ingenuity to ensure that the ever-growing band of lineside photographers did not appear in their final sequences. The locomotive travelled under its own power to and from Bedford with a Scottish crew in charge and spent much of the month of May 1964 working along part of the closed Hitchin branch for the epic British film *Those Magnificent Men in Their Flying Machines*. Here, the locomotive is seen just after arrival in Bedford shed on Saturday 9 May and before the French word 'Nord' was painted on the tender. (*S. Summerson*)

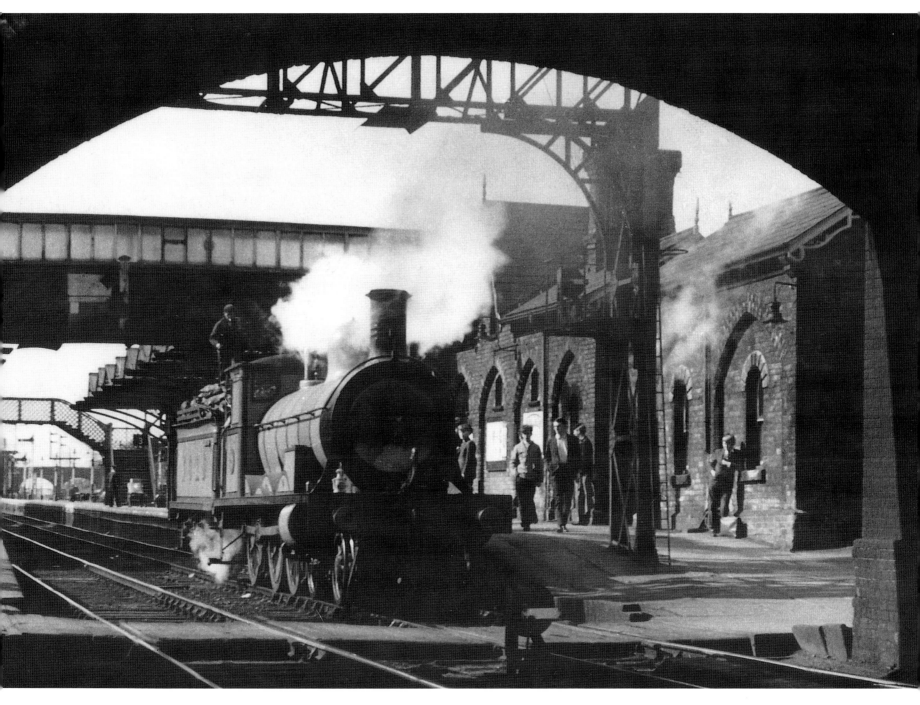

A few days after the photograph opposite was taken, No. 103 is seen through one of the arches of Ford End Road bridge taking water one afternoon at the southern end of the up slow platform of Bedford Midland Road station. The burnt smokebox door implies fairly arduous activity earlier in the day, yet the Scottish visitor seems to be attracting minimal interest from the local population. (*David Eatwell collection*)

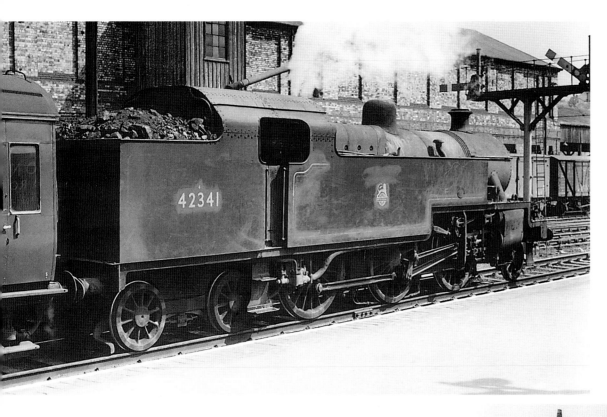

LEFT The 2-6-4T arrangement was very highly regarded by the powers that be at the LMS, and two examples of their 4Ps are shown here at Luton, but there the similarity ends because they are very different machines as can be observed. No. 42341 is a parallel boilered Fowler design which first appeared in 1927 and rapidly spread to all parts of the system. It is shown on an up local passenger train awaiting departure on Wednesday 17 June 1959. From new, the class had inside steam pipes, but most ended up as shown here after having had them moved to the outside. (S. Summerson)

RIGHT When Fairburn succeeded Stanier in 1944, the basic 2-6-4T concept was perpetuated and he wasted no time in following his predecessor's lead by having a taper boiler with top feed sitting on the same wheel arrangement on his own class which first appeared a year later. So highly was this design thought of that construction continued under BR until 1951. No. 42686 is one of these and was photographed amidst the winter snow at Luton on Monday 17 January 1955. (Harold Clements)

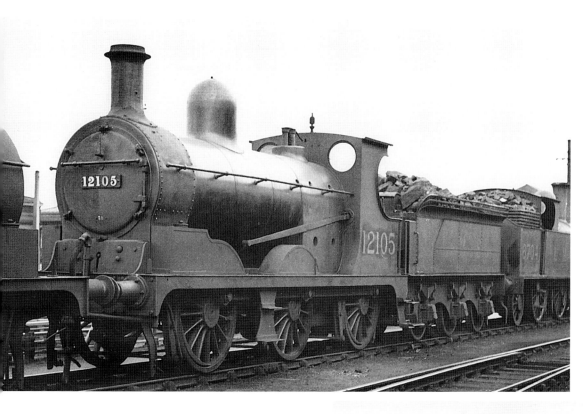

LEFT No. 12105 is one of the Lancashire & Yorkshire 0-6-0 goods engines which went to Bletchley before the war and was used mainly on chalk trains. A typical day would see it shunt the yard at Leighton Buzzard, run to Tring Cutting to pick up the chalk to take it to Tring and then return in the early evening on the fast line direct to Swanbourne Yard. All members of the class had left by 1947 and No. 12105 went to Edge Hill. It was photographed at Bletchley on Saturday 16 May 1936 and was withdrawn in May 1953. Brother 0-6-0 and another ex-Bletchley locomotive No. 12322 is preserved at Bury on the East Lancashire Railway. (*Les Hanson*)

RIGHT No. 20267 was a very handsome Johnson 2-4-0 that was built by Neilson in 1881 and was photographed at Bedford on Saturday 22 June 1935, just five months after it was renumbered from its original 267. Generally similar to the Kirtley 890 class on which they were based (see picture No. 6 in *Railway Nostalgia Around Bedfordshire*), many had Belpaire boilers and No. 20267's was fitted in 1926. They were efficient and reasonably popular machines, and were more than capable of coping with the gentle branch line work with which they were usually entrusted. (*John Dewing*)

STEAMING INTO BEDFORDSHIRE

The Standard 9F class 2-10-0s first appeared in 1954 and construction continued until March 1960 when No. 92220 "Evening Star" emerged from Swindon Works to be the last steam locomotive built for British Railways. However, not all members of the class were the same: No. 92250 was fitted with a Giesl Ejector, for example, and Nos. 92020 to 92029 were all built with the distinctive Crosti boilers. It is well known that they were heartily loathed by footplate crews at the time, chiefly because the side position of the chimney caused smoke to obscure forward vision, but partly because they were not thought of as particularly good steamers compared with the rest of the class. Another problem was internal corrosion caused by the build-up of acid deposits in the steam passages which was enough to convince authority to have them rebuilt to conform with other members of the class. All were initially shedded at Wellingborough and returned after the dreaded Crosti pre-heating boilers were removed. Unlike all the others, they were not built with smoke deflectors and somewhat surprisingly they were not provided with them after rebuilding.

Two Crostis which stayed at Wellingborough were No. 92023 (top) and No. 92027 (bottom), both photographed against that depot's distinctive shed buildings.   (TOP *S. Summerson*, BOTTOM *Les Pitcher*)

TOP RIGHT Just like the Crostis (opposite), the LMS 2-6-0+0-6-2 Garratts were another flawed type which never lived up to expectations, although here the problem was not the basic idea which was proven to be totally sound by the large number of these distinctive articulated locomotives which worked so long and so successfully in Africa and other parts of the world. No, on the LMS, failure was almost guaranteed by the Derby drawing office's insistence on having 'standard' parts (such as axle boxes) fitted instead of Beyer Peacock's own design! They were certainly a Gorton product, but they were equally an LMS failure. When new or just outshopped, they could do more than was ever asked of them, specifically on the long and heavy coal trains between the Midlands and London, but after just a few journeys performance would start to drop off and an early visit to the shops was inevitable. The hope was that they would eliminate the double-heading that was endemic on the route between Toton and Brent, and that was what they did, but it was a relief all round when Stanier's wonderful 8F 2-8-0s started to come on stream and, even later, when the Standard 9F 2-10-0s appeared. The first three LMS Garratts were built in 1927 and another 30 followed in 1930 of which No. 47988 was one, seen here at Wellingborough on Saturday 19 May 1956. Originally numbered 4988, it became 7988 during the period 1938/1939 and ended up with the number as shown in the BR scheme of 1948. Withdrawal of the class started in June 1953 and by April 1958 all had gone. Gone, yes, but lamented? … It seems not.

(S. Summerson)

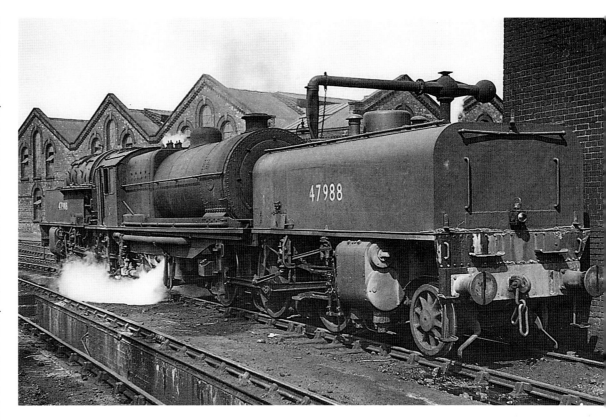

BOTTOM RIGHT This delightful little 0-4-0ST was built at Derby to a Johnson design in July 1897 with the number 1134A and was renumbered 1518 in 1907. In LMS days it retained this number and acquired the one shown under the auspices of BR. It had come to Wellingborough on loan to a quarry line in 1956 where it was photographed on shed on Saturday 2 June. Apart from brief excursions like this, it spent most of its long life based at Hasland, but towards the end it started to stray and, as the last of the class, it ended up at Lower Darwen from where it was withdrawn in February 1958. (Ken Fairey)

STEAMING INTO BEDFORDSHIRE

The same but different! Under Samuel Johnson and Richard Deeley, the Midland railway introduced one of its most successful locomotive designs in 1901 – the elegant and practical three-cylinder Midland Compound 4-4-0s. Forty-five of these beautiful machines were built up to 1909, and exactly 50 years later, with the death knell for steam having recently sounded, one of them, No. 41000, was restored in crimson-lake livery as No. 1000 to work enthusiasts' specials in many parts of the country. It subsequently went on display in the museum of British Transport at Clapham, south London, and it visited Bedford again briefly in April 1975 during its move to the National Railway Museum at York (see picture No. 266 in *Railway Nostalgia Around Bedfordshire*).

Once more it was to come out of retirement, and in the early 1980s it worked another series of specials, including two memorable winter trips over the Settle & Carlisle line (first northbound and then southbound) in February 1983 when it piloted the Jubilee class 4-6-0 No. 45690 "Leander" which carried matching crimson-lake livery. Those who braved the snow and wind to witness the spectacle on either of those days will never forget it.

Soon after the Midland Railway was swallowed up by the LMS in 1923, it was decided, somewhat surprisingly, to introduce a development of the original Midland Compound class, and a further 195 locomotives were built between 1924 and 1932. These new examples were very similar in appearance but most had left-hand-drive instead of the old Midland right-hand-drive, and some had external (bent) steam-ejector pipes out of the lower side of the smokebox. These differences are well demonstrated by the four locomotives shown at Bedford on these two pages.

Two 'genuine' Midland Compounds. No. 41038 (top) is in ex-works condition under the coal hopper on Saturday 5 January 1952 and No. 41020 (bottom) is waiting to take the 13.35 train to St Pancras on Saturday 16 September 1950.   (*R. J. Buckley*)

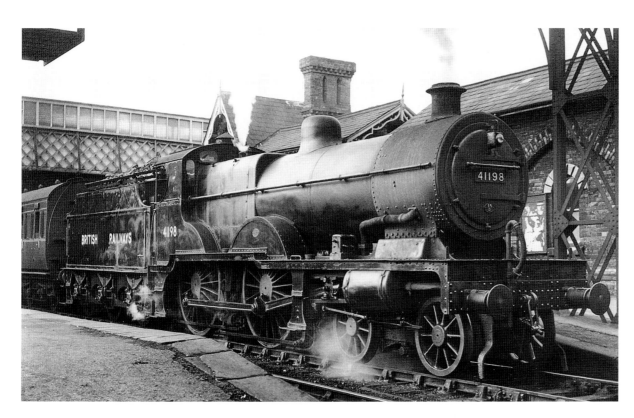

BELOW Similarly, No. 41091 is ready to depart with the 13.05 fast service to St Pancras. (*R. J. Buckley*)

RIGHT Locomotives of the old Lancashire & Yorkshire Railway were particularly appealing to those local southerners who had been brought up on a staple diet of (mainly) MR, LNWR and GNR motive power, so it was a great joy to discover interesting 'foreigners' such as No. 11353 in the area in the 1930s. This attractive 0-6-0ST was built as a tender engine by Barton Wright in 1877, but was rebuilt as seen here under Aspinall during the period 1891-1900 and given the power classification 2F by the LMS. In BR days it became No. 51353, but it was eventually displaced by standard 0-6-0Ts from Bletchley where it was photographed on Saturday 25 June 1938. *(Les Hanson)*

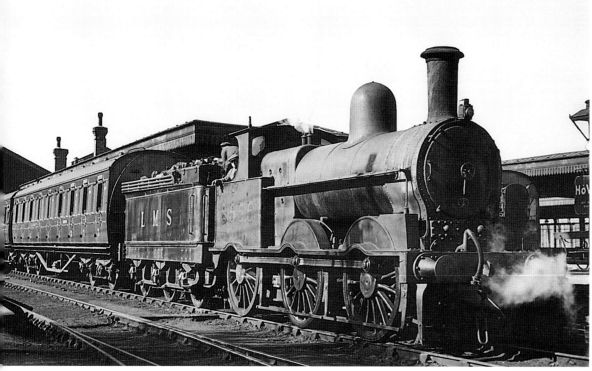

LEFT The LNWR 'Cauliflower' class 0-6-0s were introduced in 1880 under Webb and were so called because they had the company crest (said to resemble a cauliflower!) prominently displayed on the central splasher, and were the only class of 0-6-0s given this honour. One notable duty for them was to haul the afternoon school train from Wolverton to Bletchley and thus endear themselves to a generation of future enthusiasts. Four 'Cauliflowers' were at Bletchley during World War II, but all had been transferred away by the end of 1946. No. 8555 was also photographed at Bletchley on Saturday 25 June 1938, ready to haul an evening train to Banbury.

(Les Hanson)

All dressed up and somewhere to go! Decorating locomotives was something which was all the rage in the early days of railways, but only a limited number of examples were ever recorded on film for later generations to marvel at. National events such as Royal Jubilees and Coronations were often an excuse to stick flowers and branches all over the motive power, but depicted here is a far more important occasion for some of the GNR staff at Hitchin. It is the time of the 'Free Trip' for members of the Engineers' Department, as shown on the crown-topped headboard, and they are obviously intent on ensuring that as much as possible of the beautiful little 0-4-2 should be hidden from view. No. 70 was a 'Small Hawthorn' (named after its Newcastle-on-Tyne builder Messrs R. & W. Hawthorn) of 1850 and was originally one of a class of 20 standard Hawthorn 2-2-2s of which two (No. 67 was the other) were rebuilt under Stirling. *(David Eatwell collection)*

INDUSTRIAL INTERLUDE

England's only metre gauge industrial system was operated originally by the Wellingborough Iron Company which subsequently became Stewarts & Lloyds of Corby. The firm had three of these Peckett 0-6-0STs, and No. 87, illustrated at work in August 1964, is the youngest of the trio. It was built in 1942 and is shown here pushing a train of empty wagons out towards the quarry face. Note that the wagons (on the right) are carrying two skips. These could be unclipped and then lifted off the wagon by a crane so that the ore could be tipped onto the calcine clamp for burning.

(John Dewing)

Many local people will remember the two little saddle-tanks which shunted around the Royal Ordnance Factory at Elstow, during and after World War II, and will perhaps wonder what happened to them later. The answer is that they left Elstow around Christmas time 1960 to spend some months in the Cox & Danks scrapyard off Melbourne Street, Bedford (part of which is now a car park), and then they were sold on to other users. The locomotive nearer the camera is No. 1, a Hudswell Clarke 0-4-0ST of 1941 which went to a firm up in Yorkshire in June 1961, and the other is No. 6, also a 0-4-0ST, but a Bagnall of 1942 which left for Falkirk in August 1961. Both locomotives were delivered new to the R.O.F. and travellers on the adjacent Midland Main Line were often lucky enough to catch a glimpse of one or other of them, neither with a spark-arrester, pottering about amongst the stored ammunition. That there was never an explosion is something we can only wonder at today for had there been, the resultant crater would surely have rivalled those of the nearby Stewartby brickworks!

(*S. A. Leleux*)

LEFT Sentinel locomotives came in a wide variety of shapes and sizes, and were a popular unit in a number of quarries up and down the country. The type employed at Stewartby was illustrated in pictures 217 to 220 in *Railway Nostalgia Around Bedfordshire*, but as can be seen, those illustrated on this page bear no resemblance whatsoever to the 'Stewartby Type'. Here, No. 7 "Courtybella" of 1957 has perhaps the most familiar shape of all Sentinels and is shown at work in Totternhoe Quarry on Monday 27 June 1961. (*S. A. Leleux*)

RIGHT Here is something completely different. This locomotive was once a Manning Wardle 0-6-0ST named "Moltke" which was built in 1882 for work by the contractor on the Southgate & Barnet widening scheme for the Great Northern Railway and qualifies for inclusion here by virtue of the fact that it was bought by the Arlesey Brick Co. Ltd in 1894 for use in their brickworks. In 1924, the Northampton engineering firm of Blackwell & Son carried out the modification shown when they rebuilt "Moltke" with a Sentinel engine and boiler to end up looking something like this artist re-touched photograph which appeared in an original 1927 Sentinel catalogue (the chain-guards would appear to have been removed for the purposes of this illustration). It worked successfully at Arlesey until it went to the LBC at Peterborough for repair in 1946, but no work was done and it was scrapped by Cox & Danks two years later. Twenty locomotives were modified by Sentinel, the first of which was "Ancoats" (actually rebuilt by Blackwells in 1922) and which worked in Thos. E. Gray's quarries at Burton Latimer until withdrawal in 1936, although it was to survive for another 20 years before it was scrapped.

(*Robin Waywell collection*)

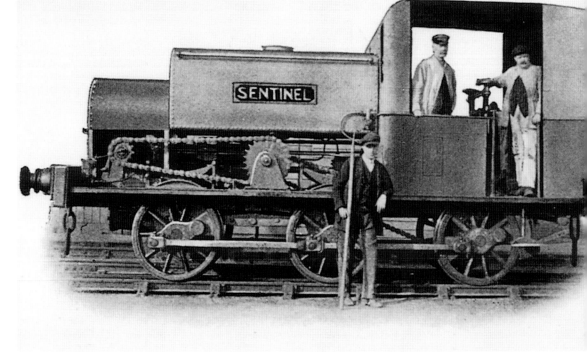

The Totternhoe chalk quarries were situated between Stanbridgeford and Dunstable North stations near the bottom of Sewell bank on the Luton to Leighton Buzzard branch, and their very existence prolonged the life of the branch in the Leighton direction for some months after the official closure date. This was so that chalk could still leave the site prior to the inauguration of the pipeline which was built to carry out chalk slurry and which did not come into use until 1965. Most lines within the quarry were standard gauge, but observant readers will have noticed a horse near the top left hand corner of this photograph, and horses were employed moving wagons on a short narrow gauge line round the other side of the kilns. Various locomotives were used on the standard gauge lines, and three of them are shown here, although much of the scene remains a mystery. The date is unknown but is probably somewhere round about 1912, and the exact identities of the two locomotives are not known either. In the main photograph, the central locomotive is thought to be a 0-4-0ST which was

built in the Cambrian Iron Foundry, Newport, by the firm of Thomas Spittle who are known to have constructed only some six locomotives between 1877 and 1899. On the right is what, at first glance, looks like a typical Aveling & Porter 'traction-engine' type of locomotive, but the position of the flywheel on the right-hand side is extremely unusual on these machines; so is this a 'pirate' copy by a different manufacturer, perhaps? The picture is obviously posed, but when? After all this time it is probable that we shall never know. The inset photograph is of a Totternhoe locomotive we do know something about because it is the Peckett 0-4-0ST of 1903, works number 947, which was transferred here from the Rugby Cement Works after the Totternhoe Lime & Stone Co. Ltd started operating the site jointly with the Rugby Portland Cement Co. Ltd in 1936. It was photographed with the 'weather-shielded cab' at rest in the quarry on Sunday 15 April 1951.

(MAIN PHOTOGRAPH *Bryan Cross collection*, INSET *John Dewing*)

The Vauxhall Motors car-building factory dominates the area to the east of the Midland Main Line just south of Luton station and adjacent to the new Luton Parkway. A major employer locally since 1905, the firm's contribution to the 1939-1945 war effort was the construction and repair of Churchill tanks, two of which are shown here on 'warflats' in this 'official' posed photograph which shows the last ones leaving the factory along the company's private sidings just off the main line. Vauxhalls had three steam locomotives at one time or another, and two of them are shown on these two pages. Above, on the tank train, is the Hudswell Clarke 0-6-0ST "C. J. Wills" of 1904 which was shown in picture No. 231 of *Railway Nostalgia Around Bedfordshire* along with their Peckett 0-4-0ST of 1936.

(*Bryan Cross collection*)

RIGHT "Kitchener" is the third of the trio of steam locomotives used by Vauxhalls, and is a 1915-built 0-4-0ST by Manning Wardle which Vauxhalls hired-in from Thomas W. Ward Ltd of Sheffield during 1953/54 (probably to cover for the absence of another locomotive under-going repairs or overhaul) photographed in the works on Tuesday 29 December, 1953. By 1954, Vauxhalls had dispensed with the use of steam on their private railway systems.

(*Harold Clements*)

LEFT "Westminster" was shown in picture No. 221 of *Railway Nostalgia Around Bedfordshire* as it was in August 1938, and it is interesting to see how little it has changed during the 13-year period between then and when this photograph was taken on Sunday 15 April 1951. In the meantime it has acquired the company's logo on the cabside, it is now in a different livery and the whistle (above the cab) has taken a little bit of a knock, but all else seems pretty much the same as it was before the war. Even the lamp bracket in front of the chimney sustains the same degree of bend in both photographs! The locomotive is a 0-6-0ST by Peckett and was built in 1914, but it was not new when it came here to the Associated Portland Cement Company's quarry at Houghton Regis, Dunstable. However, it is still in existence, and after having a good many temporary homes, at last it is gradually being brought back into working order on the Northampton & Lamport Railway.

(*John Dewing*)

SPECIAL TRAINS

In 1975 it was decided to move many of the preserved items that had once been on display at locations such as the Clapham Museum from their storage sites to the National Railway Museum in York, and a series of special trains ran down the Midland Main Line on Saturdays to bring this about. The Midland Compound No. 1000 was one local locomotive that returned to its old stamping ground when it came through Bedford on 19 April of that year (see *Railway Nostalgia Around Bedfordshire*, picture No. 266), and others are shown on these two pages. The most famous steam locomotive to be moved in this way was undoubtedly the world speed record holder "Mallard" which made the journey on 12 April, along with the LSWR Adams 4-4-0 No. 563 of 1893 (with GER No. 490's tender) and the 0-6-0T 'Terrier' No. 82 "Boxhill" of 1880 on a well-wagon. Speeds were kept to a minimum throughout and there were frequent 'comfort stops' in order to check that none of the locomotives was coming to any harm en route. Above, the "Mallard" train has just emerged from Ampthill Tunnel on the down slow line and is about to pass under Millbrook road bridge with many of Stewartby's chimneys prominent above.

(David Eatwell)

As part of the same series of locomotive moves as the illustration opposite, another famous steam locomotive was included in the train which went north down the Midland Main Line on Saturday 19 November 1977. This was the Maunsell 4-6-0 No. 30850 "Lord Nelson" of 1926 which, like "Mallard", was to be returned to steam later in order to haul a series of highly successful enthusiasts' specials, mainly in the north of England. Also part of this train was the LSWR M7 0-4-4T No. 245 of 1897 which was coupled with its bunker to "Lord Nelson's" tender and they are seen here during a brief pause in Flitwick station, at that time still complete with signal box (left). The station building itself (extreme left) has retained its classic Midland appearance despite all that has gone on around it during modernisation, but in most other aspects the previously charming station at Flitwick is totally unrecognisable today. *(David Eatwell)*

STEAMING INTO BEDFORDSHIRE

On Saturday 30 March 1994, "Flying Scotsman" began the move from its temporary home at Market Overton to new accommodation at Carnforth. It started with an early morning run up the Midland Main Line to Bedford and then a journey along the branch to Bletchley where it was to spend a couple of days to commemorate the winding-up of the borough council as the new town of Milton Keynes was about to take responsibility for the whole area. Prior to its arrival at Bedford that morning, the whole area was bathed in glorious sunshine, but as the train's arrival time approached, a Spring fog descended, and when the locomotive passed under Bromham Road bridge, it was barely visible through the mist. Its passage from Midland Road to St John's was almost totally enshrouded in murk, but thanks to a fast film and forced development, it was just about possible to achieve some sort of photographic record of the event, albeit of less than perfect quality. By the time the short train had wound its way over the Ouse Bridge and on to the St John's triangle, much of the fog had cleared, but the sunshine did not stay on the train for long and when it was due to leave, visibility had become less than perfect again! The dullness lasted for most of the journey to Bletchley, but on arrival there, much brighter conditions were the order of the day.

BELOW "Flying Scotsman" passes Lidlington. *(David Eatwell)*

ABOVE "Flying Scotsman" eases gently on to the triangle at St John's. *(David Eatwell)*

OPPOSITE "Flying Scotsman" approaches the site of the present St John's station. *(David Eatwell)*

On Saturday 8 January 1955, Workington FC were away to Luton Town in the fifth round of the FA Cup. In those far-off and happy days the railways were willing and able to accommodate special traffic. Not only that but, it is said, football supporters were well-behaved. How times have changed! Black Five 4-6-0 No. 45441 of Rugby shed works hard with its seven coaches up through the chalk cutting at Sewell towards the outskirts of Dunstable, on the last stage of its journey to Luton Bute Street. It is 12.30 and the fans will have time for a cup of tea (?) before the match! Another excursion, also hauled by a Black Five, came from Workington that day and ran into Luton Midland Road instead, but despite all this away support, Luton still won the match 5-0. *(Harold Clements)*

Jubilee on the branch! Another football special, of course, and on this occasion, Saturday 4 September 1954, Luton Town were playing Birmingham City in a First Division league match. No. 45647 "Sturdee" of Bushbury depot was the locomotive entrusted with the job of bringing the away supporters to Luton, and here it is approaching Skimpot, as it returns them in despondent mood to Stechford and New Street after the match. Unlike Rugby's unkempt Black Five opposite, the 3B men seem to have gone to the trouble of smartening up "Sturdee" for the occasion, but unfortunately their efforts were in vain as Luton won 1-0. (*Harold Clements*)

How about this for a railtour itinerary? Kensington Olympia, Willesden Junction, Gospel Oak, Harringay, Hatfield, Leighton Buzzard, Bletchley South Curve, Calvert, Aylesbury, High Wycombe, Maidenhead, Hanwell, North Acton and back to Kensington all in a fraction over five hours! The Stephenson Locomotive Society provided this feast, complete with restaurant car, on the afternoon of Saturday 12 September 1953 for 16/- (80p) a head. Standard Class 4 4-6-0 No. 75034 is seen with its train of Great Western coaches at Dunstable North. It would surely take longer than five hours to cover this ground today, even if the entire route was still open.

(Harold Clements)

On Saturday 23 February 1952, Luton Town were drawn against Swindon in the FA Cup (a match Luton won), and such was Swindon's status at the time that their supporters were able to charter no less than three special trains to carry them to Bedfordshire for the game. Thus, three of Churchward's ex-GWR 4300 class 2-6-0s (Nos. 6360 and 7300 were the other two) arrived at Luton Midland Road station that morning, and here the first of them, hauled by the smartly polished No. 6377, is shown just pulling into the down fast platform soon after 11.00, beautifully lit by the hazy winter sunshine. After the Swindon supporters had been dropped off, each 2-6-0 then proceeded to Bedford, deposited its train in sidings (either at Ampthill or Oakley Junction) and was then turned and serviced ready to collect the passengers again when the match finished. That any of these journeys received official sanction is extremely unlikely, and that there was no serious loading-gauge problem was extremely fortuitous. One observer on the recently raised platform at Luton insists that there was no more than a half inch clearance between the locomotives and the platform edge at some points as they ran in! Thank goodness the half inch was plus and not minus or one shudders to think what the consequences might have been. It is confidently stated that this was definitely the first and the last time that any GWR locomotives steamed into the area – unless you know differently, of course! (On Wednesday 20 May 1964, Castle class 4-6-0 No. 5018 "St Mawes Castle", devoid of much of its motion, was towed dead from Acton and then down the Midland Main Line to Kettering for scrap, but that obviously doesn't count, does it?) (*Harold Clements*)

It did not take long for shedmasters to discover that the 9Fs, although designed for heavy goods traffic, were pretty useful on passenger trains and were capable of surprisingly high speeds, unlike the 4Fs used previously. By 1958 their use on passenger work was fairly common. Toton shed's No. 92153, seen at Luton Midland Road, was one of nine of the class employed on Midland Division expresses on Saturday 2 August 1958, the Bank Holiday weekend. In those days there were sufficient engines and coaches available to run extra trains, and crews were glad of the overtime! No. 92153 must have done a good job that day. Four weeks later it worked a Newquay-Newcastle train forward from Bristol. *(S. Summerson)*

"The Banburian" was one of the many railtours run by Brian Lockey of the South Bedfordshire Locomotive Club in the 1950s and early 1960s. It left Luton Bute Street at 14.00 on Saturday 22 September 1962 and went via Leighton Buzzard, Bletchley South Curve and Buckingham to Banbury Merton Street. On the return journey it was the first passenger train to use the Bletchley flyover. Ex-LNWR G2 0-8-0 No. 48895 of Bushbury was allocated to the tour but failed at Bletchley and was replaced by No. 48930 of Bescot, seen here at Luton. Today's railtour operators are not always able to keep their promises of exotic motive power or unusual routes. They also charge rather more for tickets than the 15/6 (77½p!) of 1962.

(*Dave Mills*)

The sight of a Royal Scot at Leighton Buzzard would be not at all unusual on Saturday 28 April 1962; the dreaded Type 4s diesels were not in full control of the West Coast Main Line by any means and electrification was still some way off. There are two clues that this is a special working. The locomotive, 4-6-0 No. 46100 "Royal Scot" itself, bears a Nottingham (16A) shedplate, and the reporting number, 1T06, denotes a special train wholly within the London Midland Region. Whatever the reason for this train, it must have taken an interesting route if it had come from the Nottingham area.

(S. Summerson)

Stanier's 8F 2-8-0s were not confined to working goods trains as their capacity to shift heavy loads and keep them moving made them ideal for jobs like this. On 18 October 1962, No. 48385 has just passed Leagrave with a train of 20 empty coaches. The reporting number, 3T40, indicates a special working. As this was a Thursday, the coaches – over 600 tons unladen weight – are probably being positioned ready for their weekend work. Because of their lack of steam heat pipes, the 8Fs would not have worked loaded passenger trains in the winter save in an emergency.

(S. Summerson)

Most engineering trains are seen on Sundays, but not this one as 11 May 1958 was a Friday. Ex-LNWR G2 0-8-0 No. 48953 is in charge at Chaul End on the Dunstable Branch. A steel girder can be seen on the second vehicle behind the locomotive and there are two cranes in the formation. Here, and elsewhere, the railway was being called on to assist in the building of its deadly rival, the M1 motorway, but at least this line was not closed for six months, unlike the S&MJR between Ravenstone Wood Junction and Towcester! The motorway past here opened on Monday 2 November 1959. If only it were as empty now as it was then.

(S. Summerson)

In addition to the seven passenger services each way between Hitchin and Bedford daily, there were unadvertised trains for servicemen from Henlow Camp on Friday afternoons and Saturday lunchtimes. Three months before withdrawal, ex-Great Eastern J15 0-6-0 No. 65479 waits at Henlow Camp on Saturday 28 May 1960 to work the 11.30 train to King's Cross as far as Hitchin. It had hauled the empty Quad Art set tender-first from Hitchin to Shefford before crossing over and drawing forward to Henlow Camp. The return troop train reached Henlow Camp at midnight on Sundays. Let us hope the airmen travelled light as there was precious little room in the guard's van for kitbags! (*S. Summerson*)

ON SHED

To many a young (and not so young) trainspotter, the ultimate achievement was always to get round a steam engine shed without being caught and thrown out. This was an activity known as 'bunking', and the verb 'to bunk' has become well known amongst enthusiasts in this connection, although it has yet to be given this definition in dictionaries. One meaning of the noun 'bunk' in Collins is a 'hasty departure', something frequently executed on coming unexpectedly face to face with officialdom! Elderly and out of condition shed staff were no match for the legs of young 'bunkers', however, and very rarely were any apprehended successfully. One method employed occasionally to guarantee a trouble-free shed visit was to acquire a shed permit, but times, dates and visitor numbers had to be given in advance, and such details could not always be anticipated. Besides, where was the excitement in that? The staff at some sheds welcomed visitors at almost any time, whereas others would try their hardest to keep out the bunkers, all of which added to the fun of being a young trainspotter in steam days as new (and 'unofficial') paths into sheds became known, and better ways to dodge the 'difficult' staff were perfected. Of course, photographers tended to be amongst the 'not-quite-so-young' brigade and could often exude an air of respectability, thus usually making it easier to persuade staff to allow a visit. Naturally, all the photographs in this section were taken after the full and proper permission had been both sought and granted – one hopes!

The important junction at Bletchley was first given a locomotive depot in 1850 and retained one for the next 115 years. One can only speculate upon the appearance of the original building but it cannot have been very substantial because it blew down in 1872! A replacement came into use the following year and in common with many others, this one eventually had to have its roof replaced, an operation which was performed in 1953/54. Originally designated No. 3 by the LNWR, it was 2B in LMS days, then 4A for a couple of years in early BR days until in 1952 it acquired the number with which most people will be familiar today: 1E. Never a permanent home to such exotic machinery as Coronation class Pacifics, they were to be seen here on occasion, however, particularly when the passage of a Royal Train was imminent, such as on Tuesday 11 August 1964. Willesden's Coronation class Pacific No. 46240 "City of Coventry" was smartened up specially for the event and sent to Bletchley earlier on Royal Stand-by duty, but was not needed and returned home unused, no doubt to the great relief of all concerned.

(C. Stacey)

Once a major stopping place on the West Coast Main Line with a (fairly) important depot, Bletchley in its heyday was a Mecca for railway enthusiasts from far and wide. It had everything: engine shed, extensive sidings, multi-platform station, branches going off in two directions, a very impressive flyover and trains (both local and national) stopping there at all hours of the day and night. However, with the onset of diesel traction, line closures and Milton Keynes, Bletchley gradually lost almost every aspect of its former glory so that today its main purpose is to serve the (comparatively small) local population and to provide a connection to Milton Keynes, the sprawling new town of which it has become but a suburb. It is still on the WCML, of course, and has retained its railway connection with Bedford against all the odds, but it is nothing more than a faint shadow of its former self and far more trains just pass straight through now than ever deign to stop. The site of the old steam shed has become the station car park, but even as late as the end of March 1965 it was still well worth a visit, if only to admire Northampton shed's 8F 2-8-0 No. 48493 sitting quietly in the Sunday afternoon sunshine, whiling away its final hours with not a lot to do to earn its keep. Electrification was well advanced by this date, as evidenced by the overhead wire gantries clearly visible on the skyline. Bletchley shed's official closure date was 5 July 1965 (a Monday) so it had just over three months' life left when seen on this sad but evocative occasion.

(*C. Stacey*)

Hitchin shed first saw the light of day in August 1850 and delighted generations of enthusiasts with its easily visible contents for over a hundred years. From 1960, New England shed (Peterborough) supplied all Hitchin's requirements, and 34D's importance waned. A penny (1d) platform ticket gained entry to the up platform of Hitchin station and ensured a sight into the dark depths of the shed which faced the London end where only a low wall separated the entrance from spotters' eager eyes (see *Railway Nostalgia Around Bedfordshire*, picture Nos. 127 and 267). On Sunday 7 April 1946 there was a quartet of ex-GN class C1 large-boilered Ivatt Atlantics on shed which are (from left to right) Nos. 4411, 3295, 2825 and 4415, three of which are carrying their 1923 LNER numbers and one (No. 2825, was 3297) has already received its 1946 number. All four were built 1905/6 and were withdrawn between February and August 1947. The beautiful proportions of No. 4411 are shown in close-up (inset). Two similar (but not identical) Ivatt Alantics have been preserved and may be seen on permanent display in the National Railway Museum in York.

(Both photographs *H. C. Casserley*)

Hitchin shed is illustrated here in much more modern times than the photographs opposite and shows the yard with total abandonment imminent on Saturday 8 June 1963. The end of the Atlantics came with the introduction of Thompson's B1 class of 4-6-0s and here one of them, No. 61251 "Oliver Bury", is taking water where once the Atlantics had no rivals. The shed turntable has survived, however, and after being carefully dismantled, it was taken to Quainton Road (near Aylesbury) for eventual reassembly and use at this popular preservation centre. *(S. Summerson)*

Wolverton did not have a motive power department as such, but it did have a stud of remarkable old locomotives based at a shed within the works and used for internal operations. Most of these Ramsbottom saddle tanks were kept in use here for more than 60 years, as it was in 1896 that the first one arrived and it was in 1959 that the last one left. Anything other than basic servicing was carried out at Bletchley, and one or another of these unusual and fascinating locomotives was often to be seen there to the delight of spectators unable to gain access to the almost impregnable Wolverton Works. On Saturday 10 October 1954 there was an official visit to the works and the four Ramsbottom DX Special tanks (CD3, CD6, CD7 and CD8) were lined up specially for the visitors, on all of whom the sun shone brightly to make the occasion even more memorable. After all, a line-up of a quartet of 80-year-old locomotives such as these is not something one sees every day.

(*S. Summerson*)

Leighton Buzzard's shed opened in 1859 and was but a small, two-lane 'through' shed which was used mainly to stable the Dunstable branch line locomotives and those working the trains from Totternhoe quarries to Southam. In LNWR days its locomotives carried the 3L shed code, but under the auspices of both the LMS and BR it was a sub-shed of Bletchley and its locomotives carried the Bletchley shed code. After an existence of almost a hundred years it was felt that some refurbishment was required and this was carried out in 1957 – using corrugated iron! Fortunately the longevity of this material was never tested as final closure of the shed came just five years later in 1962. Ex-LNWR G2 0-8-0s (often referred to locally as 'Duck 8s') were the usual occupants in later days, and on Saturday 13 May 1961, two of them were to be seen outside. The one nearer the camera (having its coal moved forward) is No. 49287, and the other, with tender-cab, is No. 49130. The ex-LNWR Oerlikon coach on the left-hand side occupied this position for some time (see also page 166) and would be for use by the shed staff after it was no longer required on the Euston-Watford electrified lines.

(S. Summerson)

121

STEAMING INTO BEDFORDSHIRE

Wellingborough was predominantly a goods engine depot, pure and simple, with major servicing facilities for the largest goods locomotives. There was both a straight shed (opened in 1872) and two roundhouses (opened in 1867) here, as well as a concentration depot for major examinations, and although not actually on the shed site, there was a lodging house nearby (one is tempted to use the word infamous in its connection!) for loco-men who were unable to return to their home depot within the permitted hours. In the days of the LMS Garratts, many were shedded here (others lived at Toton and Hasland), and Wellingborough was one of the first depots to be allocated a Stanier 8F 2-8-0 when that class was introduced in 1935. Similarly, when the Standard 9Fs appeared in 1954, it was here that some of the first came, and Wellingborough was chosen (some say unfairly!) to be the home of all ten Crostis. But many other types could be seen here, too, and on this page are two express passenger locomotives, whilst opposite is a selection of other types common in the area.

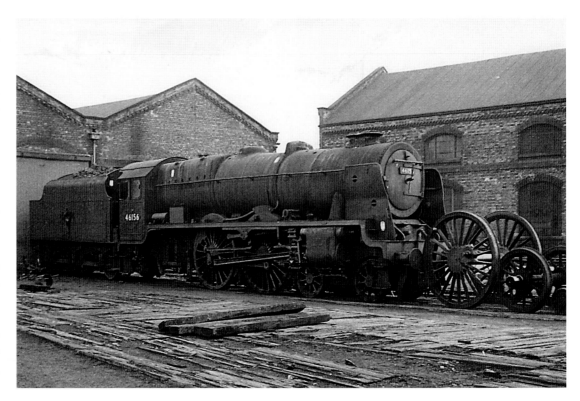

TOP RIGHT In an undated photograph, Royal Scot class 4-6-0 No. 46156 "The South Wales Borderer" has lost both its nameplate and its rear set of driving wheels, and would therefore appear to be well towards the end of its life which came with withdrawal in October 1964. Wellingborough shed itself was to last only another 16 months as its own life ended on Tuesday 13 June 1966.   (*Les Pitcher*)

BOTTOM RIGHT In another undated photograph, Jubilee 4-6-0 No. 45697 "Achilles" (with Fowler tender) still has all its wheels *and* its nameplate, but is shown in steam so perhaps it was photographed somewhat earlier than the Royal Scot above. In Midland Railway days, Wellingborough was shed No. 13, under the LMS it became 15A from 1935 and under Leicester from September 1963 it was 15B. Some of the buildings were demolished after the railway deserted them, but others still stand on what is now a busy industrial estate.   (*Les Pitcher*)

Five of Wellingborough's own locomotives were in the No. 1 roundhouse on Sunday 10 June 1962, resting between duties. Sundays were always the best time to visit sheds as they would be full to overflowing with motive power and probably not too heavily guarded! On this occasion, visitors were delighted to find the roundhouse was well lit for photography and well stocked with locomotives. From left to right they are 8F 2-8-0 No. 48763, 4F 0-6-0 No. 44574, 2P 2-6-2T Nos. 41227/4 and 8F No. 48661. The locomotives are seen across the shed turntable whose days were numbered as the whole building was demolished in July 1964. (*Ken Fairey*)

STEAMING INTO BEDFORDSHIRE

Almost unbelievably, two of Bedford's three sheds still stand – just – but how much longer they will last is a matter of constant speculation; yet stand they do, for now. The red brick two-road shed (see page 190) was opened by the Midland Railway at the time of the London Extension in 1868 and the four-road shed followed in 1886 (see opposite and page 155). The third was the LNWR shed at St John's which closed on Tuesday 1 January 1924 and which had become redundant following the amalgamation (and creation of the Big Four) the previous year. In 1894 the station avoiding line bisected the original shed and yard area, so a new connection was made when the coaling stage and turntable were added. (Surprisingly, perhaps, the latter did not become vacuum-operated until 1938.) The attractive ridge-and-furrow roof of the four-road shed was based on the LNWR style but had become so dilapidated by 1951 that it was deemed unrepairable and was replaced by the flat, concrete roof which still exists.

Last of the class at Bedford and out of use on Saturday 5 January 1952, Johnson 0-4-4T No. 58091 rests on the back coal road in the lovely low winter sunshine with the photographer cleverly ensuring that he too is included in the photograph, even if it is only through suggestion with his shadow. Also on shed, to the right, are examples of locomotive classes which were another regular sight at Bedford: a 4F and a 3F, both 0-6-0s. Dominating the skyline is W. H. Allen's office block, to the right of which is the design department from where the author's father-in-law (a long-serving senior draughtsman with the well-established firm) kept an eye on things happening around the shed for his train-mad son-in-law. 'Pop' always reckoned his 'greatest achievement' was making the phone call to announce the arrival of the yellow-liveried Jones Goods in May 1964 prior to its use in the film *Those Magnificent Men in Their Flying Machines*, and although such an occurrence could not possibly have been kept secret, Pop ensured that the local grapevine was kept extremely busy for the next couple of weeks. *(R. J. Buckley)*

There was a near sensation locally in March 1956 when the L&Y 2-4-2T No. 50646 arrived at Bedford to help out on branch line duties in the area. The operation of such a machine did not come naturally to men brought up on Midland and LMS locomotives so it saw little use during its sojourn all that way from home and spent much of its time 'stored' beside Bedford shed as it was when seen here on Saturday 1 March 1958 (MAIN PICTURE) and Saturday 19 May, 1956 (INSET). Attached to the breakdown train on the left is one of the 8F 2-8-0s which were such well-liked machines, and above the shed is the gas works which, along with almost everything else in the scene has been swept away in the name of modernisation. The shed is an exception, of course, as are the gas-holders which now are used to hold natural gas as opposed to the home-made variety which had filled them for so many years previously. Bedford shed was No. 14 in Midland days, 15D under the LMS and BR until 1958 when it became 14E. This designation lasted until September 1963 when it was changed to 14C, but this was a month after it had closed to steam so the only Bedford locomotives to wear a 14C shedplate were diesels.

(MAIN PHOTOGRAPH *R. J. Buckley*, INSET *S. Summerson*)

It is Wednesday 22 September 1965, and Bletchley shed has been officially closed to steam for more than two months, but still the ghosts of times past linger. Two 3F 'Jocko' 0-6-0Ts – Nos. 47500 and 47606 – and Standard Class 2 2-6-2T No. 84002 await removal to the scrap merchants, along with a sludge tender at the far end. Many a young enthusiast would have been very familiar with No. 47606 and would have owned a version of it as this was the 3F modelled by Triang in both 00 and TT gauge. Shortly after being seen here, No. 47500 was towed along the branch to Bedford and abandoned by the goods shed for a day before continuing its final journey to the scrapyard. Sad sights such as the one above were being repeated up and down the country as shed after shed closed at this time, and photographers were doing their best to capture such scenes before they disappeared for ever.

(C. Stacey)

The 1963 photograph here shows a real survivor undergoing repairs in Wellingborough shed. Built in 1876, No. 58182 of Coalville shed was a Johnson Class 2 0-6-0 which originally sported a round-topped boiler, but in common with most of the other 864 members of the class, it acquired a Belpaire in 1923, as can be seen. By 1963 there were just three of them left, and the last to go (in January the following year) was No. 58182 which made it British Railways' oldest working locomotive at the time. A useful life of 81 years is an achievement by any standard and a great tribute to the Victorian engineers who conceived and constructed such a durable machine. (*Les Pitcher collection*)

0-6-0T 3F 'Jocko' No. 47521 stood in Bletchley yard for some time during the early 1960s undergoing repairs to the rear wheel-set and with a rather unnecessary 'don't move' red flag attached to the bunker, but perhaps this was just the outward sign of a local railwayman's sense of humour! Introduced by the LMS in 1924, the class eventually reached 412 locomotives by the time construction ceased in 1931. They were similar in appearance and specification to the Midland Railway 3F 0-6-0Ts of 1899, although many of this series were fitted with condensing apparatus for working through tunnels in the London area. 'Jockos' were amongst the longest lasting locomotives on British Railways, and the final one did not retire from active service until 1967.

(C. Stacey)

Another pre-war view of Bedford shed's LNWR-style original ridge-and-furrow roof is shown here as a backdrop to 0-6-0 No. 3474, basking in the Saturday afternoon sunshine on 22 June 1935 and ready to answer the call to duty. Introduced in 1888 by the Midland Railway and rebuilt to this form between 1917 and 1925, this class of 3F had an inferior power rating to the 4Fs, but was generally preferred by railwaymen. Bedford was home to many 3Fs over the years, and as late as 1959 still had an allocation of 11, including No. 43474, as it had become by then. *(John Dewing)*

BITS AND PIECES

The handbills on these two pages are self-explanatory and are typical of those which the various railway companies have issued over the years to advertise their trains.

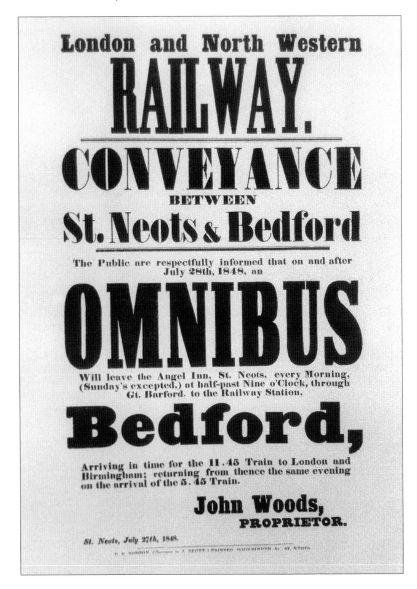

London and North Western
RAILWAY.
CONVEYANCE
BETWEEN
St. Neots & Bedford

The Public are respectfully informed that on and after July 28th, 1848, an

OMNIBUS

Will leave the Angel Inn, St. Neots, every Morning, (Sunday's excepted,) at half-past Nine o'Clock, through Gt. Barford, to the Railway Station,

Bedford,

Arriving in time for the 11.45 Train to London and Birmingham; returning from thence the same evening on the arrival of the 5.45 Train.

John Woods,
PROPRIETOR.

St. Neots, July 27th, 1848.

MIDLAND RAILWAY.
HUNTING
WITH THE
OAKLEY HOUNDS.

The Midland Train leaving King's Cross at 9.10 a.m. arrives at Bedford at 10.13 a.m., in time for the Oakley Meet.

A Fast Train leaves Bedford for London at 5.5 p.m., arriving at King's Cross at 6.10 p.m,

JAMES ALLPORT,
General-Manager.

Derby, Dec., 1866.

The LNWR bus (1848) from St Neots to Bedford pre-dated both the opening of the GNR into King's Cross and the arrival of the Midland Railway into Bedford, so the station referred to on this poster was St John's and the route was via Bletchley to Euston.

(*The De Pary's Hotel, Bedford*)

The route taken by the 'Oakley Hunt' train (1866) would have been via the GNR as far as Hitchin and the then Midland Main Line through Shefford to Bedford, although it is very doubtful if the train would be able to complete the return journey in the scheduled 65 minutes in view of the 'usual' delay inflicted on Midland trains by the GN signalman at Hitchin.

(*The De Pary's Hotel, Bedford*)

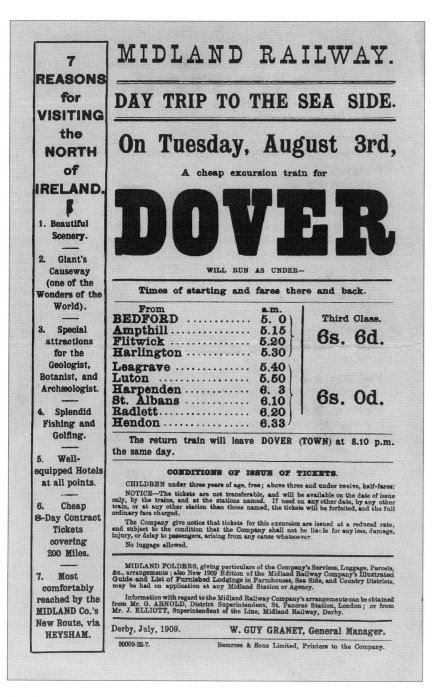

On the Dover and Nottingham handbills (dated 1909 and 1911 respectively), the fares were indeed cheap (e.g. day return Sandy/Nottingham, 20p, and Luton/Dover, 30p) and perusal of the small print extracts the unwelcome news that no luggage was allowed which presumably meant no buckets and spades on the train to Dover! Hardly worth going then really, even at that give-away price. Handbills such as these are very collectable

items in their original form and the earlier two are mounted and framed, and are to be seen hanging on the walls inside a popular Bedford hostelry, whilst the two more recently-dated handbills are in private hands. Sadly (for the owners!), none is original, and these photographs only depict reproductions, but they are no less interesting for that.

(Maurice Jeyes collection)

Two weeks before the end of regular steam working at King's Cross, Copley Hill's A1 Pacific No. 60141 "Abbotsford" approaches Hitchin with the 09.10 King's Cross Leeds 'White Rose' on Saturday 1 June 1963. Steam was to be banned officially south of Hitchin only two weeks later on 16 June, and, with the advent of electrification, virtually everything else of railway interest in this photograph went too. Even the bridge on the left disappeared in a cloud of brick-dust and rubble as it was blown up one Saturday night to allow the overhead wires to be installed at the required height.

(David Percival)

The last day of passenger services on the Bedford to Northampton line was Saturday 3 March 1962, and the honour of being in charge on such a poignant occasion fell to Ivatt 2P 2-6-2T No. 41225. Shorn of its shed-plate, this stalwart Bedford locomotive performed the same duty it had carried out hundreds of times previously, and is shown here at Turvey on that day about to push its train onwards towards Northampton. Unfortunately, the dull weather conditions which prevailed did little to raise the spirits of the many mourners who had turned out to pay their last respects to their 90-year-old friend – the 20-mile-long Bedford to Northampton branch.

(S. Summerson)

STEAMING INTO BEDFORDSHIRE

There are many different methods whereby trains are allowed to enter single line sections today and these range from radio permission to 'single train working', depending upon which line is being used and in which part of the country it is situated. Rules vary from area to area, but in steam days things were very much simpler. In most cases, the driver of a locomotive about to enter a single-line section was prohibited from doing so unless he was in possession of the single-line token (or tablet or staff) relating to that stretch of line, and signalmen at each end of the section were (in theory, at any rate!) unable to release signals allowing another train to enter until the token (or tablet, or staff) had been returned to be placed in an interlocking device which then would allow signals to be pulled off in favour of another train.

Tokens (or tablets, or staffs) were very often received, changed or given up with the locomotive on the move, and (usually) it was the fireman's duty to carry out this collection, exchange or delivery, in most cases at a point adjacent to the relevant signal box. Sure-handedness was a definite advantage because, if he dropped it or failed to collect it, the train would have to come to a dead stand and he would then have to retrieve it before he could proceed. In such an event, the reaction of the average driver would be such that the poor fireman would very swiftly learn not to be such a butter-fingers in the future!

In each of these four photographs, a token (or tablet or staff) is being exchanged between a signalman and the footplate, two at ground level and two from the signal box balcony. In some other areas, the necessity for a member of the footplate crew to hang out of the cab and be waved-at by a waiting signalman was eliminated by tablet-catching apparatus on locomotives and at the lineside, but this clinical approach was never adopted in Bedfordshire where the human touch was obviously regarded as far more reliable than any such new-fangled mechanical device.

Standard Class 2 2-6-2T No. 84006 is heading for Bedford from Northampton and the fireman is about to pass the tablet to Turvey signalman Aubrey Wilkins on Friday 15 February 1962.   (*Ken Fairey*)

Brother 2-6-2T No. 84005 is at the St John's flat crossing with a train for Hitchin on Saturday 30 December 1961 and signalman Fred Bushby stands ready to pass the tablet up to the fireman.   (*Ken Fairey*)

LEFT No. 84006 is the locomotive again, this time shown on Thursday 28 May 1959 at Irchester Junction with a train at the start of the Higham Ferrers branch and the key token being held out by the signalman ready to be collected by the out-stretched arm of the fireman. (*Ken Fairey*)

RIGHT No. 84006 is featured once more on the same train as that shown opposite (left), but this time with Olney signalman Ted Allsop leaning out of his window giving the tablet to 84006's fireman. (*Ken Fairey*)

A ride around a nice grassy site behind a beautiful model steam locomotive is something which the British public – young and old – has taken to with alacrity almost since the very first days of the railways, and it took more than world wars to stop many of these model trains from running! A selection of some modern examples is illustrated in colour on pages 188 and 189, but here is a portable system that was operating in Luton under the slogan 'Holidays at Home' during the summer of 1943. The main picture shows a 9½" gauge model of the Adams T6 4-4-0 No. 681 of 1895 in Moor Park with the location positively identified by the gas-holder in the background, whilst the inset photograph of the same locomotive is believed to be from a different occasion but a similar time, and to be across New Bedford Road in Wardown Park. Leaning on the tender is Harold Clements, a much-respected engineer of the day and a photographer of note, many of whose fascinating photographs grace the pages of both *Steaming Into Bedfordshire* and the earlier *Railway Nostalgia Around Bedfordshire*. It would be nice to think perhaps that Harold's young assistant might still recognise himself after all these years because unfortunately, as Harold is no longer with us to divulge it, the youth's identity remains a mystery.   (Both photographs *Harold Clements collection*)

In Germany, a passenger-carrying railway which runs through the streets is called a *straßenbahn* i.e. street-railway (well, logically, it would be, wouldn't it?), but despite Americans using the term 'street-car', in Britain the word 'tram' has always been preferred. Locally, the only steam-operated passenger-carrying tramway was the one which worked between Wolverton and Stony Stratford from 1886 to 1926. Locomotives on this 3'6" gauge, 2½-mile-long line came both from Germany and England, and examples of the English builders are shown here at rest in Stony Stratford.

RIGHT Photographed during the last year of the line's existence, tram engine No.2, thought to have been built by Thomas Green in 1887 and here with LMS on its side (denoting that company in place of the earlier LNWR association), is shown awaiting departure for Wolverton. It is seen at the western terminus of the line in Wolverton Road at its junction with the High Street and London Road which is behind the tram. The tall building to the left was swept away during modernisation some years ago.
(*Harold Clements collection*)

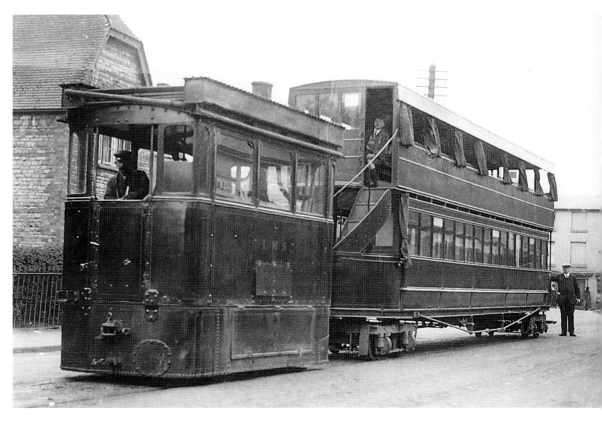

LEFT No such modernisation has taken place here, and the buildings behind the tram are largely unchanged, although their use certainly has, as most of them (the exception is the church on the right which – amazingly – seems to have retained the same iron railings to this day!) have become 'Take-Aways' providing different forms of foreign food – Chinese, Indian, etc. – for the culinary delectation of the local populace. The date of the photograph must be between 1921 and 1926 because the locomotive is the Bagnall 0-4-0ST No. 1 of 1921, and that locomotive only worked here during the last five years of the line's existence. The ugly extension to the chimney is one often seen on steam vehicles at today's traction engine rallies and is there to improve draughting. It is certainly not there for appearance!
(*Harold Clements collection*)

STEAMING INTO BEDFORDSHIRE

The interchange of tenders between locomotives, often of different classes, is something which has fascinated those observers (now often referred to irreverently as 'rivet-counters') interested in minutiae ever since tender-swapping became such a common practice. To the inobservant, such changes went unnoticed, but it would be a very inobservant viewer indeed who did not notice that right from the date of issue, some Jubilees carried tenders which were patently different from many others, and in all, four different types of tender were used, although not all of them were new.

Jubilee class 4-6-0 No. 45612 "Jamaica" was one of a short series of Jubilees (45607-45616) originally fitted with a Fowler 3,500-gallon tender with high straight sides, but this was later changed to the version shown here; the low-sided 3,500-gallon Fowler tender. The third variety was the 3,500-gallon type with high curved sides, but most (although by no means all) Jubilees ended their lives with the Stanier 4,000-gallon tender (as illustrated on pages 18 and 19 for example), as did so many larger locomotives of LMS origin.

In this photograph, Jubilee class 4-6-0 No. 45612 "Jamaica" (of Kentish Town shed) is seen pausing at Luton with a local train for St Pancras on Saturday 13 June 1959. (*S. Summerson*)

Two more locomotives with straight-sided tenders are shown above at Leagrave on Monday 20 April 1953, but both of these are somewhat older than the Jubilee opposite. On the left is Horwich 'Crab' 5F 2-6-0 No. 42771 (class introduced in 1926) doing a bit of shunting around the yard; and carrying express passenger headlights as it hurries through the station with a northbound train is No. 41074, a member of the LMS version of the Midland Compound 4-4-0 4P class which was introduced in 1924.

(*Harold Clements*)

Stanier's masterpiece was the Princess Coronation class of Pacifics (to give them their correct title) which first appeared in streamlined form in 1937 and which eventually extended to 38 locomotives, the last but one of which (No. 46256 of 1947) was named after the designer himself: "Sir William A. Stanier, F.R.S." Various nicknames were applied to the class over the years from 'Streaks' and 'Semis' through 'Coros' to the totally inaccurate name 'Duchesses', but whatever they were (or are) called, and in whatever form they appeared, there can surely be no denying that they were as handsome a class of locomotive as ever appeared on a British railway. The original streamliners had their casings removed in time, and from 1938 new members of the class appeared in conventional (i.e. unstreamlined) form, like No. 46251, "City of Nottingham" (of Crewe North shed) which is shown here with just over two years of its life left as it passes through Leighton Buzzard station on Sunday 3 June 1962. Three Coronations have been preserved, the best known of which, No. 46229 "Duchess of Hamilton", has since travelled many thousands of miles hauling enthusiasts' specials. The other two are No. 46235 "City of Birmingham" which moved to a new home within that city at the end of 2000, and No. 6233 "Duchess of Sutherland" which was returned to steam during the summer of 2001.   (S. Summerson)

The Britannia class Pacifics were the first of the Standard classes to be introduced and originally took to the tracks in 1951. Building continued until 1954 and the class extended to 55 locomotives, all bar one of which (No. 70047) were named. Britannias were originally fitted with hand-rails on the top and leading edges of the smoke deflectors, but following an accident which occurred near Didcot in 1955, the blame for which was restricted visibility, the hand-rails were removed from those working on the Western Region, plus most of the others. Hand-rails were then replaced by hand-holes, some of which are clearly visible in this photograph. No. 70028 "Royal Star", now of Edge Hill shed, is seen here as it heads south and passes through Leighton Buzzard station with an express goods train on Saturday 28 April 1962.   (S. Summerson)

LONDON AND NORTH WESTERN RAILWAY.
NOTICE.
EXTRACT FROM 8 VIC. CAP. 20, SEC. 75.
"IF ANY PERSON OMIT TO SHUT AND FASTEN ANY GATE SET UP AT EITHER SIDE OF THE RAILWAY FOR THE ACCOMMODATION OF THE OWNERS OR OCCUPIERS OF THE ADJOINING LANDS, AS SOON AS HE AND THE CARRIAGE, CATTLE, OR OTHER ANIMALS UNDER HIS CARE, HAVE PASSED THROUGH THE SAME, HE SHALL FORFEIT FOR EVERY SUCH OFFENCE ANY SUM NOT EXCEEDING FORTY SHILLINGS." BY ORDER.
EUSTON STATION.
1ST NOVEMBER, 1884.

Ex-Great Eastern J19 0-6-0s were not noted for their frequent or regular appearances in the Bedford area, but the odd one or two did make the occasional foray with a goods train from Cambridge, sometimes working right through to Oxford, and here is one of these chunky machines, No. 64688, returning from there on Monday 16 May 1955. St John's No. 2 signal box is behind the train and the fireman will just have collected the miniature staff to allow the train to enter the first of the single line sections between here and Sandy. At Willington, the miniature staff will be exchanged for a full-size version for the section to Blunham, when another full-size staff will grant passage as far as Sandy station where double track recommences for the remainder of the journey to Cambridge. The location above will be recognised by many of today's cyclists because the bridge still crosses over the River Great Ouse here and is near the start of the current cycle track between Bedford and Great Barford, most of which closely follows the track-bed of this former LNWR branch. The footbridge shown on the right (to the front of the locomotive) also still crosses the river at this point, but so does the 'new' road, Longholme Way, on a sweeping curve behind the footbridge and rather dominates the scene now. (*John Gibbs*)

INSET This oddly worded notice was attached to a gate near the spot shown in the main photograph. (*John Gibbs*)

Since their introduction by the LMS in 1945, Fairburn's 4P 2-6-4Ts were a common sight on both the main lines and the branch lines of Bedfordshire, as indeed they became over much of the country both north and south of London. Powerful and elegant, they were masters of their work, and even a goods train as lengthy as the one in this photograph would not cause the slightest strain. The photographer is standing on the end of the up platform of Hitchin station, looking north, and the satisfyingly long southbound goods train from Bedford has just come off the former Midland Main Line (later to become but a humble branch line of mainly single-track) to join the East Coast Main Line. It was here during much of the 1860s that the Great Northern signalmen took such delight in delaying the Midland Railway's trains, the result of which was the construction of the London Extension through Luton and St Albans in 1868, and the building of the truly magnificent St Pancras station as a snub to the much less grand King's Cross station next door. Bedford shed's No. 42174 with its nicely shining tank-side is seen as it passes the Great Northern's goods sheds at Hitchin on Saturday 6 July 1963, some 18 months after the closure (to passenger trains) of the branch from Bedford.

(*S. Summerson*)

Black Five 4-6-0s were among the few steam classes still working on that fateful day in August 1968 when BR ran their last advertised standard gauge steam-hauled passenger train, the infamous 'Fifteen Guinea Special' over lines (including the Settle & Carlisle) in the north-west of England. (The 1'11½" gauge Vale of Rheidol was actually BR's last steam operated service, and continues in use – though no longer under BR ownership – to the present day.) Right from the introduction of the Black Fives in 1934, it was realised that Stanier had designed a real winner, which is why eventually the class extended to 842 engines, and it was only fitting that some of them should last right through to the very end of steam working on British Railways and why so many have been preserved. When No. 45048 was photographed here at Bletchley on Wednesday 5 May 1965, there were still more than three years to go, but the local shed would be closed within a couple of months and, as can be seen, full electric operation was imminent (power to the overhead lines was actually switched on in the Bletchley area on Monday 19 July 1965, exactly two weeks after the official closure of the shed). It was not only to be the end of steam working, of course, it was to be the end of an era and the end of a way of life for a large slice of the population.

(*Ken Fairey*)

BRITISH RAILWAYS.

London Midland Operating Area.

SPECIAL NOTICE

THIS NOTICE MUST BE KEPT STRICTLY PRIVATE AND MUST NOT BE GIVEN TO THE PUBLIC.

NOTICE TO DRIVERS, GUARDS, SIGNALMEN AND OTHERS RESPECTING THE INTRODUCTION OF STANDARD :—

PASSENGER AND FREIGHT TRAIN CLASSIFICATION
HEADLAMP CODES and
BLOCK BELL CODES.

COMMENCING JUNE 5, 1950

J. W. WATKINS,
Operating Superintendent.

E.R.O. 23967

BRITISH RAILWAYS
LONDON MIDLAND OPERATING AREA
PASSENGER AND FREIGHT TRAIN CLASSIFICATION

On and from Monday, 5th June, 1950, a standard classification for passenger and freight trains will be introduced and from that date the headlamp and block bell codes shown on page 44 of the former L.M.S. General Appendix (pages 19 and 20 of the Cheshire Lines Appendix) will be superseded by the following :—

Classi-fication	Engine Headcode (white lights or discs)	Description of Train	Block Bell Code	
			Beats on Bell or Gong	How to be given
A		Express passenger train, newspaper train or breakdown van train or snow plough going to clear the line or light engine going to assist disabled train, or fire brigade train proceeding to a fire. Officers' Special train not requiring to stop in section	4	Consecutively
B		Ordinary passenger train, mixed train, or breakdown van train NOT going to clear the line, or loaded †rail motor train or fire brigade train NOT proceeding to a fire. *Branch passenger train	4 / 4	3 pause 1 / 1 pause 3
C		Parcels, fish, fruit, horse, livestock, meat, milk, pigeon or perishable train composed entirely of vehicles conforming to coaching stock requirements ... ... Express freight, livestock, perishable or ballast train piped fitted throughout with the automatic brake operative on not less than half of the vehicles... Empty coaching stock train (not specially authorised to carry 'A' headcode), or empty †rail motor train	5 / 5 / 5	1 pause 3 pause 1 / 3 pause 1 pause 1 / 2 pause 2 pause 1
D		Express freight, livestock, perishable or ballast train partly fitted with the automatic brake operative on not less than one third of the vehicles	5	Consecutively
E		Express freight, livestock, perishable or ballast train partly fitted with not less than four braked vehicles connected by vacuum pipe to the engine... ... ... Express freight, livestock, perishable or ballast train with a limited load of vehicles NOT fitted with continuous brake	5	1 pause 2 pause 2
F		Express freight, livestock, perishable or ballast train NOT fitted with continuous brake.	5	3 pause 2
G		Light engine or light engines coupled ... ... Engine with not more than two brake vans	5 / 5	2 pause 3 / 1 pause 1 pause 3
H		Through freight or ballast train not running under class 'C,' 'D,' 'E,' or 'F' headcode.	5	1 pause 4
J		Mineral or empty wagon train	5	4 pause 1
K		Freight, mineral or ballast train stopping at intermediate stations ... ... *Branch freight train ... ... Freight, ballast or Officers' Special train, requiring to stop in section	3 / 3 / 7	Consecutively / 1 pause 2 / 2 pause 2 pause 3

*—To be used only where authorised by the Operating Superintendent.
†—The term "Rail Motor train" includes "Push and Pull train" and "Motor train."

The classification of each train will be shown in the appropriate column of the Working Time Table on and from Monday, 5th June, 1950.

The 'description of train,' e.g. Fitted freight No. 1, Fitted freight No. 2, Express freight ✠, shown in the Summer 1950 Freight Working Time Table will remain during the period of this Time Table only.

Euston Station,
May, 1950

J. W. WATKINS,
OPERATING SUPERINTENDENT.

BR (LM) loco headcodes and block bell codes.
(*Bill Davies collection*)

AROUND THE COUNTY IN COLOUR

Sharnbrook Tunnel was constructed to relieve the 1 in 119 gradient northbound and the 1 in 120 gradient southbound between Sharnbrook and Irchester on the Midland Main Line to ease the journey of the long and heavy goods and mineral trains that for so many years laboured along this route from the Midlands to London. However, with the introduction of Leicester power box, the tracks through the tunnel have been singled and are much less used today. In the photograph above, on the left are the lines which take the 'easy' route through Sharnbrook Tunnel and on the right is the pair which surmounts the summit. Seen in June 1961, Black Five 4-6-0 No. 44852 of Leeds Holbeck shed carries the express-goods head code and is working well as it hurries up the 1 in 119 incline with a train of fully braked box vans and conflats for the Midlands.

(Michael Mensing/Colour-Rail)

In this photograph, Sharnbrook Tunnel runs (more or less) under the bank seen above Leicester shed's Black Five No. 44667 as it heads for home during the evening of Saturday 30 August 1958. This 4-6-0 is on the down fast line with a stopping train of very mixed stock and is approaching Sharnbrook Summit, much to the relief of the fireman who will be able to take a bit of a breather over the next four or five miles before he has to start work again to tackle the next natural obstacle – nearly 15 miles of almost unbroken climb up to Desborough. *(Trevor Owen/Colour-Rail)*

The first water troughs to come into use on the Midland Railway were opened at Oakley, 3¾ miles north of Bedford, in 1904, and they remained in use for the next 60 years. To make the most of them it was vital that the scoop be lowered at the right time – too early might cause damage and too late could result in not enough water being taken which might mean an extra stop having to be made to top up; not a popular option! Here, the white-handkerchief-headed fireman is leaning out of the cab of Kentish Town's Jubilee class 4-6-0 No. 45622 "Nyasaland" at the start of the troughs as the express train for St Pancras keeps up to the speed necessary to lift the water into the tender. The date is the summer of 1960.

(*David Eatwell*)

Once the main line from Bedford to St Pancras was electrified, steam specials were banned there because of a perceived (but non-existent) problem with running under the wires, and although such specials are far from regular, they are now permitted. Such locomotives as "Green Arrow", "Taw Valley" and "Flying Scotsman" have all shown their faces along the line at one time or another, some more than once, and on Saturday 22 April 1995, it was the turn of Black Five 4-6-0 No. 44767 "George Stephenson" to go through. The weather in Bedfordshire at the time was definitely not conducive to meaningful photography, but after a water stop at Kettering the spring sunshine broke through and cast its light upon this grand spectacle of the train tearing past the closed station at Glendon and Rushton as it worked its way up the 1 in 97 of this part of Desborough bank.

(David Eatwell)

On Saturday 19 September 1964, the Locomotive Club of Great Britain (LCGB) ran one of their ever-popular rail tours out of St Pancras. Called the Pennine Limited, it followed a somewhat circuitous route and took in Stamford, Peterborough, Sheffield (Victoria), Stockport, Crewe (including the Works), Stoke, Derby (Friargate), Nottingham (Victoria), Aylesbury and Marylebone. The locomotive used to top and tail the trip was Royal Scot class 4-6-0 No. 46155 "The Lancer" of Crewe North shed, an engine not normally seen on the Midland Main Line. Other motive power used on the Pennine Limited that day included the Peppercorn A1 Pacific No. 60128 "Bongrace", Black Five No. 45382, 2P 2-6-2T No. 41229, and Horwich Mogul No. 42772. They certainly don't run 'em like *that* any more! Bearing a gaudy yellow stripe on its cab-side (indicating a ban on its use south of Crewe!), "The Lancer" is at Oakley, just north of Bedford, and the reason for this choice of photographic location is the imminent demise of the tall semaphore signals, due for demolition in just a couple of day's time. Although closed to all traffic since September 1958, Oakley station buildings still stand and some of them have been in use as a garage (and vehicle repair depot) for most of the intervening period.   (*Ken Dickens*)

Not one of the most frequently photographed branch lines was that which connected the two county towns of Bedford and Northampton, but an unfortunate accident near Turvey on Saturday 31 July 1960 did attract a certain amount of interest from photographers. The driver of 8F 2-8-0 No. 48616 of Cricklewood shed misunderstood the signalman's instruction, and instead of drawing forward just a short distance as had been intended, the loco-man set off for Northampton with his train-load of lengths of track believing he had the right of way. Unfortunately he was on the road used to store a line of unwanted rail vehicles and collided with them at a fair old speed with the predictable results shown here. Not surprisingly the 8F was written off, but it took three months for BR to come to the conclusion that it was unrepairable! *(Ken Fairey/Colour-Rail)*

Kirtley-designed, Derby-built. The occasional pre-war colour photograph of a steam locomotive surfaces from time to time and we are fortunate indeed that at least one of them (of a double-framed 2-4-0) was taken outside Bedford shed in 1938. When they first appeared in 1866, these 156 class locomotives worked secondary expresses along the Midland Main Line, but by the time this photograph of No. 20012 was taken in 1936, much more mundane duties would be the order of the day, such as comparatively gentle trips along the Kettering-Cambridge cross-country branch line. No. 20012 was built in November 1867 and was withdrawn in March 1945 from Kettering depot, but keeping up with the almost unbelievable series of number changes it underwent during its 77½ years of life is little short of miraculous. When new, its number was 110 and this was changed to 110A in June 1879. In April 1889 it became No. 20 and in May 1892 this was altered to 20A which lasted until November 1894 when it was replaced by 157 and then 157A in August 1896. From November 1907 it carried the simple number 12 and received the number seen here in April 1934, all of which must be something of a record! Besides being allocated such a string of different running numbers, it also carried three different boiler types during its life. The original was replaced by a C from December 1882 and this in turn with a B in December 1897.

(Bill Davies collection)

R. A. Riddles' wartime design of Austerity 2-8-0s was rightly renowned, to the extent that some 733 locomotives of this class were eventually constructed from 1943 for use throughout the railway system. By this evening in August 1964, when the above photograph of No. 90395 heading north out of Bedford with a train of coal empties was taken, scrapping of the class had been in progress for five years or so, and by 1967 all had gone. And gone means *really* gone because, somewhat surprisingly, not one was saved for preservation. The view is that looking south from Bromham Road Bridge, but how different it is today! The site of the carriage sidings is now the station car park, although a single storage line for electric trains has been retained, and empty coaching stock is stabled in a new location south of the modernised Bedford station which is 100 yards or so closer to Bromham Road than the original. (*Ken Dickens*)

This is a view that was captured from Ford End Road Bridge, Bedford, during the evening of Saturday 8 September 1962 and is the exact opposite of the one on the facing page. Here, Jubilee class 4-6-0 No. 45579 "Punjab" is passing Bedford's tall coal hopper and motive power depot as it speeds northwards with an express train on the down avoiding line as another heads for London on the up. Much of the area on the left is now occupied by a modified layout, installed when Bedford's rebuilt station opened in 1976, and where the parked wagons are is now the sidings used for storing electric units. *(S. Summerson)*

By standing on the coaling level of Bedford's coal hopper (but not the top – perhaps the photographer suffered from vertigo), this is the scene that was caught by the camera on Sunday 10 January 1960 and is full of interest. Ford End Road Bridge, from which the photograph opposite was taken, stretches from the right-hand side of the shed roof to the right-hand edge of the photograph. On the left, wagonloads of coal are waiting to be emptied into the coal hopper and behind them is a 3F 0-6-0. Wellingborough shed's 8F 2-8-0 No. 48365 is prominent in the centre and on the right can be seen new ballast on the down fast line which indicates that re-laying is in progress, a fact borne out by the red and yellow mechanical shovels and the 600 Hillman van. Between the shovels (with a boiler-suited worker walking past) are two curved rails which will be used to replace those on which the turntable runs in the turntable hole. At the water column on the right is an Ivatt 2-6-2T (perhaps No. 41271 or No. 41272) and between the loaded coal wagons and No. 48365 is the ash-pit above which locomotive fires are cleaned and smokeboxes emptied of ash. Other locomotives are scattered about the site as was usual on a Sunday, but come tomorrow, this scene of peace and tranquillity will be one of hustle and bustle as the working week begins. *(Colour-Rail)*

With the driver looking nonchalantly out of his cab, Royal Scot class 4-6-0 No. 46133 "The Green Howards" of Kentish Town shed comes off the Bedford avoiding line and heads for St Pancras with an express train during the summer of 1960. Bedford shed's coal hopper is just visible through the smoke under the gantry and the position of the signals above indicates that there is soon to be a train in the opposite direction which also will take the avoiding line that ran 'round the back' of Midland Road station when this photograph was taken. Today a new platform on the down avoiding line of Bedford's rebuilt and resited station has speeded things up considerably by eliminating many crossing-movements and leaving the other platforms free to deal with the frequent electric trains to London and beyond.

(*David Eatwell*)

The two separate bores of Ampthill Tunnel were always attractive to photographers, more particularly in steam days and most particularly of trains going south as the tunnels have a gradient of 1 in 200 against those travelling in that direction. The 8F shown on this page has just emerged from the original 1868 bore with one of the enormous coal trains from Toton to Brent which these locomotives so willingly took over to supplement the work of the problematical LMS Garratts. The lines to the left are the fast lines which use the 1895 bore and came into use when the route was quadrupled at that time. *(David Eatwell/Colour-Rail)*

Steam was due to be replaced on the Midland Main Line by April 1961, yet this photograph of Royal Scot class 4-6-0 No. 46162 "Queen's Westminster Rifleman" arriving at Luton with an up express around 13.00 on a June day of that year shows that the diesels were not yet in control. But No. 46162's work on the Midland was almost done and within a month it had left Kentish Town shed for further duty at Saltley (Birmingham). By October 1961, the diesels' Achilles heel had been discovered – their train-heating boilers were useless! Run-down steam locomotives were pressed back into service, but the Scots would not be seen at Luton again too often.

(*J. P. Mullett/Colour-Rail*)

Wartime photographs of trains in action are a comparative rarity, and colour photographs even more so because of the slow speed of colour film at the time and, although film was never actually rationed, national security must also have been a factor. Nevertheless, the photographer of LMS Jubilee class 4-6-0 No. 5608 "Gibraltar" approaching the stop at Luton station with an express for St Pancras obviously had not let either of those 'minor inconveniences' deter him. In view of the upturned collar on the thick coat being worn by the gentleman nearest the camera, it was probably the depth of winter, and the direction of the lengthy shadows implies the afternoon. "Gibraltar" was a long-time resident of Leeds Holbeck shed which could mean that this was a Leeds-London train, but all that is pure speculation as no more details of this rare view have survived. The photographer was an American serviceman who was stationed nearby, and this remarkable photograph was donated to the present custodian by his family.

(Colour-Rail)

STEAMING INTO BEDFORDSHIRE

Snow had fallen in the Luton area over the Christmas holiday period in 1962, and with the full service restored by the 28th, what was more natural than to brave the elements and go out to photograph some of the trains that glorious afternoon? Christmas Day was a Tuesday that year so by the Friday of the same week both passenger and goods trains were running more or less normally, and one of each is shown on these two pages.

One of the passenger trains that stopped at Luton on its way to St Pancras was hauled by the disgustingly filthy Jubilee class 4-6-0 No. 45650 "Blake" of Derby shed, so it is just possible that Derby is where this train came from.

(S. Summerson)

One of Wellingborough depot's rebuilt Crosti 9F 2-10-0s, No. 92027, storms through Luton with the usual long train of coal empties from Brent to Toton. An abiding memory of the time is how run-down many locomotives were allowed to get during the latter days of their life.

(*S. Summerson*)

STEAMING INTO BEDFORDSHIRE

For some time during the mid to late 1960s, the London Railway Preservation Society kept a small collection of standard gauge steam locomotives (most of them industrials) at Skimpot on the Luton/Dunstable border, and a couple of them are shown here as they were on Sunday 5 March 1966. The first to come was the Metropolitan 0-4-4T No. L44 (not illustrated) which travelled to Skimpot in steam from Neasden in March 1964.

RIGHT The LRPS's second locomotive was "Swanscombe" and is an early Andrew Barclay 0-4-0ST (it was built in 1891) which arrived from the Thurrock Chalk & Whiting Co. Ltd, Essex, in February 1966. It was not often steamed at Skimpot, so this photograph is something of a rarity. It moved on to its present home at Quainton Road in May 1969 and was the last locomotive to leave the site.

(Harold Clements)

LEFT "Sydenham" is an Aveling & Porter (a sort of traction engine on rails, see also page 99) of 1895, and went from Kent to be looked after by the Enfield & District Veteran Vehicle Society. It came to Skimpot in September 1965 to be followed by a lengthy sojourn at Quainton Road until September 1997 when it was moved to the Chatham Dockyard Historic Trust on long-term loan for eventual restoration.

(Harold Clements)

The goings-on at Dunstable North station were always something of an anachronism and are perfectly demonstrated in this photograph. Hatfield shed's N7 0-6-2T No. 69704 has just arrived with a train from Luton but will be going no further in this direction. Those passengers wishing to continue to Leighton Buzzard will already have walked across the platform and changed trains, and the contents of the parcels van are in the process of being transferred over to the waiting train. All this is because rival companies had originally built and operated the two lines (the LNWR from Leighton Buzzard and the GN from Welwyn through Luton), and the original antipathy between them was never really resolved. However, there was always one daily through service in each direction (out from Leighton Buzzard about 07.30 and back from Luton about 08.30) but travellers at most other times of the day had this enforced train-change across the platforms at Dunstable North. It came as no surprise, therefore, that Beeching decided to give this pleasant little line the chop, and all services finally ceased on 26 April 1965.

(Colour-Rail)

STEAMING INTO BEDFORDSHIRE

Bedfordshire is not particularly well served by private steam railways, and in fact there are none at all to standard gauge anywhere within its boundaries. Nevertheless the county does possess a couple of narrow gauge lines which are shown on these two pages. The most visited is undoubtedly the 2'6" gauge line within the confines of Whipsnade Wild Animal Park (or Whipsnade Zoo as it is still popularly known), but only a very small proportion of visitors will go there specifically and solely for the railway. The animals, birds, reptiles, etc. are obviously the main draw, but once inside the grounds, visitors in their droves flock to travel on the steam railway, and at peak times a wait before boarding is often necessary.

On Sunday 17 September 1978, the locomotive on duty at Whipsnade was "Excelsior", the 1908 Kerr Stuart 0-4-2ST that had come to Whipsnade when the Bowaters paper factory in Kent had no further use for it. The black swans beside the line are obviously quite impervious to the steaming monsters which regularly disturb their peace. *(David Eatwell)*

RIGHT Bedfordshire's only freely accessible steam-operated narrow gauge railway is shown as it was on Saturday 7 September 1991 when one of the locomotives working trains that day at Leighton Buzzard was the smart little 0-6-0T "Doll". Andrew Barclay built the 2' gauge "Doll" at their works in Kilmarnock in 1919 and it came to the railway from Bressingham where it had been on display for a few years previously. The correct name of the locomotive is "Doll" as shown in the photograph (right), but whilst at Bressingham it acquired a pair of cast nameplates off a scrapped locomotive called "The Doll", but that was never the locomotive's proper name. (*David Eatwell*)

BELOW This photograph shows "Doll" with the wrong nameplates soon after its arrival at Leighton Buzzard. (*Harold Clements*)

It was the usual practice for passenger trains using the branch to Dunstable North from Leighton Buzzard to have their locomotives running 'right way round' in order to go smokebox first up the 1 in 40 of Sewell Bank, although push-and-pull trains would have the locomotive at the rear when travelling in that direction, of course. Thus, trains returning downhill would normally have their locomotives in the 'wrong way round' mode.

Above, the locomotive with so much steam to spare is Ivatt 2-6-2T No. 41289 and is shown leaving base-station Leighton Buzzard for Dunstable on Thursday 10 May 1962. Beside it, also with a little surplus steam is 8F 2-8-0 No. 48657, patiently waiting to take its long train further north, down the West Coast Main Line.   (*J. P. Mullett/Colour-Rail*)

On a lovely sunny summer's day at Leighton Buzzard, BR Standard Class 4 No. 75028 does some shunting with its mixed goods train around the station yard on Tuesday 30 July 1963. Some of this class of 4-6-0s were fitted with double chimneys, no doubt in an attempt to improve their perfor-mance, but such appendages most definitely did not improve their appearance. Ironically, the locomotives whose numbers span No. 75028 (i.e. Nos. 75027 and 75029) are both preserved, but not No. 75028 itself. *(S. Summerson)*

Summer Saturdays always held an extra interest for trainspotters in steam days, mainly for the reason depicted above – one just never knew what one was likely to see next. Winter Saturdays had their football specials which brought unusual motive power into unusual areas, but other special trains were easy to organise (unlike today!) and were popular with the punters, so they were likely to be seen almost anywhere at almost any time. Crewe North's Royal Scot class 4-6-0 No. 46134 "The Cheshire Regiment" is the locomotive at the head of the Evereds Social Club special heading towards London and seen south of Bletchley in the summer of 1960. One can only speculate at the fun the social club members were having on their train, and would be having when they reached their destination.

(David Eatwell/Colour-Rail)

Stanier 8F 2-8-0 No. 48149 waits patiently for the road at the southern end of Bletchley station on Saturday 13 April 1963 with a goods train for the London area. Prominent against the skyline on the left is the Bletchley flyover which was built at enormous cost in 1959, but which was usually referred to as the 'White Elephant', not only because of its size and colour, but also because very quickly it came to be realised that it was a complete waste of money as so few trains ever used it. Should the East-West rail-link between Oxford and Sandy/Hitchin ever become reconstructed, perhaps the Bletchley flyover will justify its cost at last, but until that unlikely day, the name 'White Elephant' seems set to stick. (*S. Summerson*)

The drab and unkempt appearance of most steam locomotives in their wartime black livery was something that observers had become all too used to during the 1939-45 conflict, and this condition was something which inevitably persisted well into the post-war austerity period. By 1948, however, things were beginning to look up a bit, and the newly nationalised railways needed to emphasise their existence by gaining as much favourable publicity as possible. One obvious way was to smarten up the locomotive stock but, sadly, not too many locomotives actually gained from this commendable policy. One that did, however, was the rebuilt Patriot 4-6-0 No. 45540 "Sir Robert Turnbull", newly out-shopped in experimental green livery but not yet fitted with smoke deflectors and seen here coming in to Bletchley one evening in July of that year.

(H. N. James/Colour-Rail)

RIGHT The history of the LNWR 0-8-0 tender engines is one of the most complicated of any type to have run on British rails, so suffice it to say that No. 9162 was a G1 class locomotive of a type which extended to some 502 examples, although because of rebuilds, modifications and conversions, not all were ever in service at the same time. As late as 1955, 275 0-8-0s of this type remained in use, but from then onwards numbers swiftly declined as more and more of the standard classes were issued. Still with its round-topped boiler, No. 9162 was photographed outside Bletchley shed between duties in June 1938, and as we admire the classic lines of this elegant locomotive, we can be most thankful that the photographer had gone to the trouble (and expense!) of putting some colour film in his camera.

(*Les Hanson/Colour-Rail*)

BELOW Also on Bletchley shed but on Saturday 5 June 1965, some of Stanier's finest await the call to duty. Prominent is Bletchley's own Black Five 4-6-0 No. 44837 and to the right is Northampton's 8F 2-8-0 No. 48360. (*Harold Clements*)

Willesden's unrebuilt (and un-named) Patriot class 4-6-0 No. 45547 was often to be seen on the West Coast Main Line in 1960 and a small number of these handsome locomotives worked both here and on the Midland Main Line (through Bedford and Luton) at the time. They sometimes piloted expresses and sometimes took their turn on slow and semi-fast passenger trains, but here one is doing what they most often did at the time, i.e. hauling a fitted goods train. That none still exist is regarded as one of the major gaps in the British steam locomotive preservation movement. The location of the above photograph is between Wolverton and Bletchley (Milton Keynes fills this area today) and the train shown is heading for London.

(*David Eatwell*)

In the summer of 1960, the down 'Caledonian' left Euston at 15.45 on weekdays and was due to arrive in Glasgow some 7¼ hours later after a single stop (at Carlisle) at an overall speed of just under a mile a minute. Today, electric trains are scheduled to do the journey in under five hours, but for all the modern efficiency, the romance has surely gone.

ABOVE A regular performer on the 'Caledonian' in the summer of 1960 was Carlisle Kingmoor's Princess Coronation class Pacific No. 46226 "Duchess of Norfolk", and it is seen here passing through the pleasant Buckinghamshire countryside which today has become the sprawling conurbation of Milton Keynes. (*David Eatwell*)

RIGHT Later that year, Coronations were still in charge of the 'Caledonian', and on Friday 16 September 1960, No. 46236 "City of Bradford" took its turn at the head of this prestigious train, also seen here in the region of the present Milton Keynes. (*Harold Clements*)

More has been written and more photographs have been taken along the Bedford-Bletchley branch line than any other in the county for the very good reason that it has always been a particularly attractive operation. Originally opened as the Bedford Railway in 1846, it was eventually incorporated into the Oxford-Cambridge line and after Beeching it was the only part of that important cross-country route to remain open, although the section from Bletchley to Oxford does survive (much of it mothballed). Against all the odds, Bedford-Bletchley is still operative today and is frequently visited for its continued use of traditional signal boxes, semaphore signals and manually-operated level crossing gates. The M1 motorway which was opened in 1959 crosses the line just west of Ridgmont station, and in this photograph Standard Class 5 No. 73013 has just passed underneath the road with an unfitted goods train heading in the Bedford direction on Saturday 17 October 1964. The 4-6-0 has already lost its front number plate and, along with most other steam locomotives as electrification progressed, the smokebox door lamp-bracket has been lowered for safety reasons. *(J. P. Mullett/Colour-Rail)*

The first station out from Bletchley in the Bedford direction is Fenny Stratford which was noted for the unusual configuration of its staggered platforms until 1948 when the down platform was rebuilt opposite the up platform in conventional style. The station is situated but a stone's throw from the Watling Street which crosses over the line a few yards to the west on the bridge seen above the train in this dramatic photograph. The locomotive here is one of Thompson's celebrated B1 class 4-6-0s, No. 61287 of Cambridge, and the train is pulling away from Fenny Stratford on the last leg of its journey with the 07.37 train to Bletchley on Saturday 18 March 1961. The 4-6-0 will then go on to Bletchley shed for watering and turning before making its way back with a train later in the day. Towards the end of the steam era, Eastern Region locomotives became a common sight at Bletchley and one could very often be seen on shed adjacent to the West Coast Main Line, patiently awaiting its repatriation to more familiar country. (*Bill Davies collection*)

It was on Saturday 5 October 1963 that the Midland & Great Northern Joint Railway Society special train 'The Wandering 1500' came along the Hitchin branch to Bedford during its exhaustive 233-mile-long day excursion, and here it is making a dramatic restart after pausing for a few minutes for the road on the bridge over the River Great Ouse. Originating at Broad Street, the train took passengers through Finsbury Park, Bedford, Northampton, Stratford-upon-Avon and Rugby before returning them to base late in the day, tired but happy. Happy is more than can be said for the B12 4-6-0 No. 61572, however, because it started off far from well and its condition gradually worsened during the day. It was withdrawn immediately afterwards and sat in the yard at Norwich for some time awaiting its fate, but all turned out well in the end with its return to steam on the North Norfolk Railway in 1994.   (*S. Summerson*)

Even in diesel days, double-heading was a way of life on the former Midland Railway, but one never did expect to see 9Fs going around in pairs! It is March 1959 and Nos. 92153 and 92156 are in Bedford yard. The train is one of several run at that time to test the braking capability of these fine machines on loose-coupled wagons. Later it was to set back and continue northwards, a whole episode which went totally unremarked in the railway press of the day. The photographer worked at Rugby Testing Station and would have been at the scene on official business. Some guys have all the luck! Most structures in this scene have been consigned to history, but exceptions are the footbridge to the left of Ouse Bridge signal box (on the right-hand side of the photograph) and one or two of the old lines which now are dead-end sidings used for the occasional storage of unwanted rail vehicles. The line on the far right is presently used by trains on the Bedford-Bletchley route.   (*John McCann/Colour-Rail*)

On parts of the East Coast Main Line (including the southern section), the two centre tracks are the fast lines and the outside tracks are the slow. However, on Sunday 19 June 1962, reballasting was taking place near Huntingdon where some strange sights were to be seen, and this is one of them. 9F 2-10-0 No. 92186 has occupancy of the up fast line at the head of the slow-moving ballast train, thus necessitating A4 Pacific No. 60006 "Sir Ralph Wedgwood" to take to the slow in order to pass with its express for King's Cross. The up slow line at this point was rationalised at the time of electrification and removed, but subsequent events may have caused a rethink. Reinstatement has therefore become a distinct possibility.

(*Tommy Tomalin*)

Potton station was built in 1862 and was always one of the more attractive 'country' stations to be found anywhere on the whole of the line between Oxford and Cambridge. There was (and still is) a good view of it to be had from what was the road bridge just to the south, but that is not where the photographer was standing on this occasion. He was on the station foot-bridge to capture Bletchley's Fairburn 2-6-4T No. 42069 just as it trundled in with a train from Cambridge back to base in April 1960. The line closed at the end of 1967 and virtually everything apart from the station building itself has disappeared. Today it is a smart and well-kept private residence.

(*F. G. Cockman/Colour-Rail*)

Saturday 25 June 1960 was a typically busy day on the East Coast Main Line and, as usual, southbound slow trains were being held just north of Sandy station in order to allow fast trains to pass. This was because there were only double track running lines through the old Great Northern part of the station at the time, which was something that also occurred a few miles further south at Arlesey. Even today on the same line there is only a single pair of lines running across Welwyn viaduct and despite the parallel Hertford Loop, hold-ups still persist which have prompted thoughts of a new viaduct to the east to carry extra lines. Above, 9F 2-10-0 No. 92201 waits for the road at Sandy and is passed by B1 No. 61075 on its way to King's Cross with an evening passenger train. (*Tommy Tomalin*)

Britannia class Pacific No. 70041 "Sir John Moore" sweeps through Sandy and heads for King's Cross one morning during the summer of 1961. Along with many other class members, No. 70041 had for some time been shedded at Norwich Thorpe, mainly to work expresses to Liverpool Street, but because of the arrival of diesels on the Great Eastern Main Line, the Britannias became surplus there and were subsequently re-allocated. Seven (of which No. 70041 was one) went to Immingham shed (near Grimsby) and the rest made the short journey to March in Cambridgeshire. Another Britannia, No. 70013 "Oliver Cromwell", was one of the locomotives to haul BR's 'Farewell to Steam' 15-guinea special on Sunday 4 August 1968 and it, along with class leader No. 70000 "Britannia", have passed into preservation.

(*Michael Mensing*)

Sheer elegance. Peppercorn A1 class Pacific No. 60145 "Saint Mungo" of Gateshead shed speeds through Sandy with a southbound express train in 1961. It can only be surmised why not a single member of this class of beautifully proportioned locomotives was preserved, but there is a strong possibility that a brand new A1 will be working again in the near future. When it appears, No 60163 "Tornado" will have been constructed completely from scratch in Darlington and will be the first standard gauge main line steam locomotive for domestic use to be built in this country since "Evening Star" emerged from Swindon Works in March 1960. As usual, another train is being held under the footbridge (right), waiting to nip out on to the fast line between up expresses. (*Michael Mensing*)

Towards the end of 1959, V2 No. 60853 of New England (Peterborough) shed heads for home territory and steams purposefully below the Sandy sand-hills after just restarting a stopping train from King's Cross. This class of mixed traffic 2-6-2s extended to 184 examples and was designed by Gresley to be introduced in 1936. Rightly or wrongly, its members were known as the engines which won the war, but Black Five supporters have been heard to dispute such a title strongly. This is quite an unfortunate location in railway terms as over the years more than one derailment has occurred very close to this spot. The one best remembered by local residents involved a refrigerated-van train from the north that left the tracks just here in 1964. Well, the good folk of Sandy couldn't allow all that fresh fish to go to waste now, could they?   (*David Eatwell/Colour-Rail*)

The rather complicated itinerary of the four locomotive six-coach SLS (Stephenson Locomotive Society) special which ran on Saturday 14 April 1962 was detailed in the captions to pictures 270-273 in *Steam Nostalgia Around Bedfordshire*, and here the train is seen at Hitchin on a day which was blessed with beautiful weather throughout. The Fowler 2-6-2T No. 40026 of Bedford shed has just arrived at Hitchin from its home base and will shortly hand over the train to Capt. Bill Smith's lovely little green-liveried J52 0-6-0ST No. 1247 to travel a short distance up the East Coast

Main Line and then return to Luton along the Hatfield branch. The train originated in Birmingham, was double-headed for some of the legs, and besides the places already mentioned, took in the Leighton Buzzard branch through Dunstable as well. There were some interesting light-engine movements too, but it does not take much imagination to guess the reaction of authority should such a tour be proposed in this day and age.

(*Jim Jarvis*)

RIGHT This is the third of the trio of pre-war colour photographs to find its way into the present volume. It is of one of the celebrated GN small-boilered 4-4-2 Atlantics and was caught on shed at Hitchin in 1937. Built at Doncaster in June 1902 with the number 996 on its works plate, it originally carried the running number 252 and was renumbered to 3252 by the LNER. They classified this series as C2, a class which somehow managed to acquire the nickname 'Klondykes', probably because of the 'Gold Rush' which was happening in the Yukon at about the time the class was being introduced.

(*Bill Davies collection*)

LEFT Here is a member of an equally renowned (in some quarters!) class of locomotive: this Midland 3F 0-6-0 was rebuilt in 1924 from an original which first saw the light of day as far back as 1891. No. 43342 will have just worked along the branch from Bedford with some sort of goods train and is on Hitchin (GN) turntable being prepared for the return. The date is Saturday 2 March 1963. (*S. Summerson*)

185

STEAMING INTO BEDFORDSHIRE

Two 1960 views of the south end of Warden Tunnel with trains heading for Hitchin are shown here and feature two types of locomotive which saw much service from Bedford shed up to the very end of steam operations.

In this photograph taken from the road bridge (which still exists), Ivatt 2-6-2T No. 41272 (caught a few yards further on from where No. 43428 is in the photograph on the right) was in front of the single coach which is what passenger trains on the branch had degenerated to by that time. The locomotive was something of a local celebrity as it was the 7,000th to be built at Crewe and bore plaques on its sides to this effect. It came new to Bedford in September 1950 and was eventually re-allocated to the West Country.

(*David Eatwell*)

From track level, 3F 0-6-0 No. 43428 is seen bursting out of the the tunnel with a short goods train.

(*Fred Cockman/Colour-Rail*)

In May 1964, the preserved 4-6-0 Jones Goods locomotive No. 103 (built by Sharp Stewart of Glasgow in 1894) steamed all the way to Bedford from its home in Scotland to feature in sequences of the epic British comedy film *Those Magnificent Men in their Flying Machines*. It spent much of its time working along the recently-closed branch from Bedford to Hitchin, and is seen here near the hamlet of Ireland between Southill and Shefford stations. The story is told in greater detail in the caption to photographs Nos. 275 and 276 in *Railway Nostalgia Around Bedfordshire*. (*Colour-Rail*)

STEAMING INTO BEDFORDSHIRE

Bedfordshire (and its environs) may not have any 'full size' preserved steam railways, but over the years there has been no shortage of miniature lines using live steam in the area, and four of them are shown on these two pages. Some lines have come and gone, unfortunately, and amongst them are those which once ran in the grounds of Woburn Abbey, in The Moor, Luton, in the gardens of the Royal Oak and White Horse public houses at Cardington and Southill respectively, in a farm field beside the Midland Main Line at Radwell, in Mill Meadows in Bedford and behind the Rose public house in Cotton End, just to mention a few. Those illustrated are at Summerfields Farm, Haynes (2½", 3½", 5" and 7¼" gauges), at Willen Lake, Milton Keynes (7¼" gauge), in Ferry Meadows, Peterborough (10¼" gauge), and the White Horse public house, Southill (7¼" gauge), although the last mentioned is another of those which has gone in recent years. Also available to lovers of working model steam locomotives is the short line behind the Fancott Arms, near Toddington (7¼" gauge), which is a fairly recent installation and is a great pleasure to sample (along with a nice cooling pint!) on a balmy summer evening, although in common with others of these lines, not all the trains will be steam hauled here. (See also page 136.)

RIGHT TOP Willen Lake, Milton Keynes in May 1994.
(*David Eatwell*)

RIGHT BOTTOM Summerfields Miniature Railway, near Haynes, in September 1998.　(*David Eatwell*)

ABOVE Ferry Meadows in August 1989.   (*David Eatwell*)

RIGHT Southill in August 1994.   (*David Eatwell*)

STEAMING INTO BEDFORDSHIRE

Steam returned to the Bedford-Bletchley Branch on Saturday 21 December 1996 after much forward planning by the Bedford-Bletchley Rail Users Association and the overcoming of innumerable difficulties. The eight-person organising committee was chaired by Capt. Bill Smith and, amongst other luminaries, contained the BBRUA Chairman Richard Crane. Four return trains for the public were scheduled, but a last-minute hitch at Bletchley resulted in the cancellation of the first train of the day (and thus the balancing return). The Severn Valley Railway's Standard Class 4MT 2-6-4T No. 80079 was the motive power, and on one of the coldest days in living memory, what was left of the event took place in virtually unbroken sunshine.

The locomotive is watered in front of Bedford's old Midland Railway engine shed during a rest between trains in the morning.
(*David Eatwell*)

The last public train of the day leaves Bedford for Bletchley as the evening sun descends. A private trip for 'staff' ran after dark and was almost as well patronised as the earlier trains had been. It was certainly enjoyed as much. (*David Eatwell*)

During the night of Saturday and Sunday 15 and 16 December 1990, Black Five No. 44932 and Standard Class 4 2-6-4T No. 80080 were diesel-hauled from Butterley to St Pancras for a filming session at the London terminus. Soon after midnight the train paused at Bedford to allow the steam locomotives to take water in the yard, and the small group of waiting photographers was absolutely delighted when, by arrangement, the cl 47 diesel pulled forward to allow this unspoilt view. Sadly, the St Pancras scenes were never used in the finished film, whilst the estimated cost (loss?) of the whole exercise to 20th Century Fox was reported to be some £100,000!

(David Eatwell)

191

INDEX